LEFT: Among the many changes seen over the last 50 years have been both a decline in the numbers of small shunting locomotives and also in the volume of tank traffic on rail. On October 28, 1994 Class 08 No. 08953 heads a rake of vinyl chloride monomer tanks through Barry Docks on the last leg of their journey from the ICI works at Burn Naze, near Fleetwood, to the European Vinyl Corporation's unloading siding at Barry.

MAIN COVER PICTURE: Class 66 No. 66134 heads 4F01, the 10.46 empty stone train from the Tarmac terminal at Pendleton (Brindle Heath) to Mountsorrel, through Salford Central station on September 5, 2019. This train runs once or twice a month bringing granite from Mountsorrel.

MAIN PICTURE INSET: The opening of the Channel Tunnel in 1994 brought a considerable boost to intermodal traffic and Class 90 No. 90133 heads 4A13, the 13.10 SO Trafford Park to Wembley, through Stafford on September 22, 1997.

Contents

AUTHOR:
David Ratcliffe

PRODUCTION EDITOR:
Sarah Spencer

DESIGN:
Craig Lamb
Kriele Ltd
design_lamb@btinternet.com

COVER DESIGN
Jake Sidebotham

PUBLISHER:
Steve O'Hara

PUBLISHING DIRECTOR:
Dan Savage

COMMERCIAL DIRECTOR:
Nigel Hole

ADVERTISING MANAGER:
Sue Keily

ADVERTISING EXECUTIVE:
Craig Amess

MARKETING MANAGER:
Charlotte Park

ISBN:
978-1-911276-87-6

PUBLISHED BY:
Mortons Media Group Ltd,
Media Centre, Morton Way,
Horncastle,
Lincolnshire,
LN9 6JR.
Tel: 01507 529529

PRINTED BY:
William Gibbons and Sons,
Wolverhampton

COPYRIGHT:
©2019 Mortons Media Group Ltd.
All rights reserved.

The Changing Face of Railfreight

The railway scene in Britain has undergone considerable change since the 1970s and nowhere has this been more evident than in the freight sector. Here methods of operation have been adapted to respond to an increasingly challenging financial environment, while the balance of commodities carried by rail has fluctuated in response to the underlying adjustments in the country's wider economy as it has moved from one based on industrial production, to a service consumer model. This change has included the gradual disappearance of wagonload traffic, plus in recent years the dramatic collapse of coal carryings, but other sectors such as chemicals and metals have also waned in line with changes in manufacturing. On a more positive note, there has been considerable growth in general merchandise flows, now mostly carried in containers, while construction-related traffic has seen steady growth and departmental freight workings have gained in significance.

Accompanying, and in part driven by, these developments, the freight enthusiast has also witnessed the almost complete replacement of both the locomotive and wagon fleets, and while most freight trains have become noticeably longer than they were 30 or 40 years ago, they are now far fewer in number, with some parts of the network devoid of any freight other than the occasional departmental working.

In 1974 upwards of 7800 freight trains, including local trip workings, were running each day, but by 2003 this figure had fallen to just over 1100, while at the same time the number of active locations (including both private sidings and BR depots and freight sidings) that regularly received or despatched traffic had declined from a little more than 3,000 to less than 300, with almost all the survivors being private sidings.

The BR wagon fleet also contracted, being reduced from more than 200,000 in 1973 to no more than 21,200, in terms of its post-privatisation equivalent, by 2004. Redressing the balance somewhat, the average wagonload more than quadrupled in the same period, while most wagons were also being used much more intensively than had been the case in the 1970s.

Consequently, the overall freight tonnage carried by rail has declined more gradually, from 175 million in 1973/74 to 138 million in 1986/87, falling to around 117 million in

2013/14. The subsequent loss of most coal movements meant that in 2017/18 overall freight tonnage was recorded at some 75 million conveyed by an average of just over 600 freight trains a day, yet despite this decline there is still much in the modern railway scene to interest the dedicated freight follower.

Any work of this nature would not have been possible without the kindness of numerous railway employees whom, over the last 30-plus years, have generously allowed me access to yard and freight depots, while thanks must also go to many fellow enthusiasts for their assistance and support. In that regard a special mention is due to Trevor Mann, Hywel Thomas, Roger Silsbury, Dave Millward, John Edser, Geoff Corner, John Dedman, David Hayes and Paul Shannon, all of whom have allowed me to include photos from their collections, and to Paul Bartlett, Mark Saunders, Peter Fidzcuk, David Larkin, David Monk Steel, Bob Wallace, and Simon Bendall, as well as Tony Johnson, Phil Pollard, and the rest of the Casey Lane crew for providing much useful information.

David Ratcliffe
2019

Today almost all freight traffic is conveyed by block train while the locomotive fleet is now dominated by the General Motors-built Class 66 with more than 85% of all freight workings booked for Class 66 haulage. Still in its original EWS livery Class 66 No. 66161 heads north at Crewe Basford Hall Junction on May 21, 2019 with a Southampton Eastern Docks to Halewood train comprised of empty STVA single-deck car carriers.

LEFT: In contrast, for much of the last half of the Twentieth Century wagonload freights could be seen across the entire network, entrusted to a wide variety of different locomotive types. The unique Brush Traction 2,880 bhp prototype Class 53 locomotive No.1200 'Falcon' crosses the River Usk Viaduct just east of Newport Station with 9F61, the local wagonload trip from the East Usk branch to Newport Alexandra Dock Junction Yard, in April 1974. Immediately behind the locomotive is an empty Algeco 40-tonne ferry tank, on the first leg of its return journey to the continent after making a delivery of silicon tetrachloride to the Monsanto chemical plant at East Usk, while the train also included a 16-tonne Mineral and a number of empty Tube wagons. *(©Colour-Rail)*

CHAPTER 1

It's a Wagonload World

In Britain over the last half century mixed freight services have had a somewhat eventful history. In 1968 almost 70% of all freight traffic fell into this category, but by 2018 such trains were almost non-existent, replaced by container and block workings. A legacy of the steam age, when the rail network reached into almost every corner of the country, wagonload freight involved moving goods from their originating point to destination by a series of trains, with the consequence that wagons might spend hours, sometimes days, in a marshalling yard awaiting an ongoing service.

British Rail's 1955 Modernisation Plan had sought to address some of the inefficiencies of this system with the closure of small yards and freight depots, while in 1963 the *Beeching Report* had recommended transferring as much traffic as possible into block trainloads or, where such was not viable, switching lower volume freight flows to the newly planned Freightliner container service. However, despite the report wagonload freight continued, but with its rolling stock for the most part comprised of out-dated, short-wheelbase and low capacity wagons, the railway increasingly struggled in the face of growing road competition to retain any significant share of the general merchandise market.

Prior to the publication of the *Beeching Report* there had been more than 5,000 public goods terminals and station goods yards open

for general freight use, although some 78% of all traffic they handled went to just 855 of these locations. Consequently there followed a significant cull and the 1974 copy of the *TOPS Location Handbook & Wagon Forwarding Guide* listed just over 760 BR-owned sidings, depots or terminals as still open for general freight use. However, these were located throughout the network, with almost as many to be found in rural areas as in the towns and cities, therefore the range of the traffics they handled varied considerably, as did the volume of business found at each. For instance, to the north of Inverness along the Kyle of Lochalsh and Far North lines, could be found some 18 BR sidings and depots open for coal and general merchandise, while on the Cambrian Coast line, from Shrewsbury to Aberystwyth and Pwlheli, there were still nine active BR freight locations handling traffics such as domestic coal, fertiliser, animal feed and commercial explosives. However, such extravagant provision eventually came under scrutiny and in the run up to the withdrawal of its traditional wagonload freight services, which was implemented in 1983/84, BR closed more than 70% of its freight sidings and depots, retaining only those that could be easily served by the new air-braked network.

Finally, in the early 1970s BR had been able to invest in a fleet of new air-braked opens and vans with which to launch a number of

new high-speed Air Braked Network services capable of running at up to 75 mph, with the ABN freights only stopping en route to detach or attach pre-marshalled portions. By 1977, when the Air Braked Network was rebranded as Speedlink, some 50 services were either planned or already running, while the government had authorised investment in a further 3,400 air-braked wagons. Encouraged by BR's commitment to a modernised wagonload service, the private wagon industry, both in Britain and abroad, also began to develop new vehicles, most notably the 80-tonne glw bogie ferry vans which with a capacity of 57-tonnes provided a considerable boost to cross-Channel freight flows.

Inevitably though as the Speedlink network grew, it began to resemble the earlier wagonload operation for, while the traffic may have been switched from smaller unfitted or vacuum-braked wagons into larger air-braked vehicles, the service was still reliant upon a considerable number of local trip workings to feed them into the long-distance trunk trains. Some of the older hump yards may have been closed but the remaining Speedlink Network hub yards still saw plenty of shunting activity as local trips were broken up and their wagons remarshalled. With operational costs rising, in 1986 Speedlink ceased to use Ashburys yard in Manchester and in January 1987 the Harwich to Zeebrugge train ferry closed with all cross-Channel traffic then concentrated on the Dover to Dunkirk sailings.

Later that year, Speedlink also pulled out of the yards at Severn Tunnel Junction and York Dringhouses. Following the sub-sectorisation of BR's entire freight operation, in 1987 Railfreight Distribution was given responsibility for both Freightliner and Speedlink but, when a detailed analysis showed that Speedlink was losing some £30 million on an annual turnover of £45 million, the decision was taken to withdraw the service with effect from July 8, 1991.

However, this was not to be the end for wagonload as five daily mixed freights continued running between Dover and the yards at Bescot, Cardiff, Crewe and Willesden in an effort to retain as much continental traffic as possible prior to the opening of the Channel Tunnel in 1994 and around 50 private sidings and freight depots retained their rail connections to handle this traffic.

Sadly many other flows previously moved by Speedlink were lost to road and although a handful were able to be recast as block train workings, most of these new Rfd Contract Services as they were known proved to be short-lived.

In the 1960s and 1970s domestic coal was still widely used for household heating and it remained the mainstay of most local trip workings, but the other traffics such freights handled depending on each area's economic activity and customer base. On September 20, 1967 Class 24 No. D5009 heads 8T47, the 07.03 from Llandudno Junction, past Betws-y-Coed on its way up the Conwy Valley with a Flatrol MJ wagon which was on its way to the nuclear power station at Trawsfynydd immediately behind the locomotive. The Flatrol MJ was carrying a discharged nuclear flask, returning to Trawsfynydd from the British Nuclear Fuels reprocessing plant at Sellafield, while the rest of the train comprised one 21-ton and 10 16-ton Mineral wagons all loaded with domestic coal which were en route to the busy coal depot at Blaenau Ffestiniog. Since many of the Mineral wagons were unfitted a Brake Van has also been marshalled at the rear of the train. (© RCTS collection)

Enterprise

In 1994 Transrail, one of the shadow freight franchises established in the run up to privatisation, took the unexpected decision to reintroduce a mixed freight Anglo-

In the early-1970s local freights were still a common sight throughout the country and traffic for the Windermere branch was handled by Trip 46, the daily 12.35 departure from Carnforth to Burneside, pictured being shunted in Kendal goods yard by Class 25 No. D7620 on April 28, 1972. In earlier years the expansive goods yard at Kendal had received a wide variety of goods including agricultural equipment, animal feed, fertiliser, bricks and concrete pipes, as well as tank wagons of fuel oil and kerosene, but by 1972 deliveries of domestic coal, and the occasional van loaded with commercial explosives for the local quarries, were its main traffic. In addition the trip also regularly conveyed industrial coal, carried in 13-ton Hopper wagons, to Cropper's Paper Mills' private siding at Burneside located some two miles north of Kendal. However, this was to be one of the last workings of Trip 46 for at the end of April it would be withdrawn prior to the rationalisation of the branch line in the run up to the electrification of the West Coast Main Line north of Preston. *(© RCTS collection)*

LEFT: Like many local freights the Conwy Valley trip would only run as required, and as such it did not feature in the Working Timetable but instead was listed in the area Trip Notices booklet.

No.47 CLASS 24 DIESEL
(Included in Freight Train Bonus Scheme)

	arr	MO	dep	
Llandudno Jn. HS			06 35 LD	0T47
Llandudno Jn.	06 40			
		MSX		
Bangor		B	06 07 LD	0T47
Llandudno Jn.	06 28			
		SX		
Llandudno Jn.			07 03	8T47
Llanrwst	07*30 C		07*46	
Blaenau Ffestiniog	08 32		10 08	Propel
Trawsfynydd	10 49		12 21	
Blaenau Ffestiniog	13 02		13 15	
Llanrwst	pass		13 50	
Llandudno Jn.	14 15	A		

A – Locomotive works in Multiple 15 53
Llandudno Jn. to Holyhead TWThO
16 05 to Chester DD MFO.
B – Locomotive off 01 35 Pcls from Guide
Bridge.
C – To work to DCE's instructions when
not required at Trawsfynydd or
Blaenau Ffestiniog

Scottish service branded 'Enterprise' that quickly catered for a mix of traffics including anthracite, china clay slurry, cider, starch, salt and timber. The number of 'Enterprise' services, both along the WCML and on other parts of the rail network, would increase following railfreight privatisation in 1997, with English Welsh & Scottish Railways keen to encourage new business. Unfortunately however the combination of an economic downturn and corporate changes within EWS saw its enthusiasm for wagonload freight soon diminish. In 2009 EWS was acquired by Deutsche Bahn AG which, in the face of increased competition from new railfreight operators like GBRf and DRS, chose to concentrate its focus on its more profitable bulk trainload flows and the last of the wagonload workings were gradually allowed to wither away.

The traditional vacuum-braked wagonload freight remained a common sight in most parts of the country until the early-1980s and in April 1982 Class 27 No. 27010 is pictured at Craiglockhart Junction, coming off the chord to Slateford Junction, with a Mossend to Millerhill working. Such trains invariably carried a lot of domestic coal with 21-ton Hopper wagons conveying anthracite and phurnacite from South Wales destined for Edinburgh's Haymarket and Portobello coal depots, as well as 16-ton Minerals en route to the coal depots at Bathgate, Perth and Ratho. *(© Colour Rail)*

While coal provided the bulk of westbound Trans-Pennine freight traffic, by the 1980s scrap metal was one of the major commodities to be seen heading east. On May 17, 1983 Class 40 No. 40060 slowly trundles through Manchester Victoria with 8E84, the 09.12 SX Warrington Walton Old Junction to Healey Mills, passing Class 25 No. 25276 which is standing on the "Wall Side" road, the usual home of the locomotive assigned to banking duty. Once the train has cleared the points, the Class 25 will emerge and buffer up to the rear of the freight in order to assist the Class 40 up the stiff 1-in-59 incline to Miles Platting. The long raft of 16-tonne Minerals marshalled behind the Class 40 are carrying steel scrap from Lowton Metals in Ashton-in-Makerfield and the Central Wagon Co. at Wigan Springs Branch.

With more than 230,000 being built between 1950 and 1958, the 16-tonne Mineral was far and away British Rail's most numerous wagon type. In addition to carrying coal, they were often used in steel scrap traffic and two unfitted 16-tonners, TOPS code MCO, are pictured when loaded with shredded scrap at Sheffield's Tinsley Yard in June 1980.

Class 33 No. 33045 had a single 21-ton Mineral wagon in tow when spotted arriving back at Basingstoke with 6L79, the 14.00 SX from Farnborough in March 1982. Unsurprisingly the Corrall's coal depot at Farnborough would close later in the year.

Until the year-long miners' strike of 1984 coal was also the main commodity conveyed by the vacuum-braked wagonload freights that ran from Healey Mills to either Ashburys Yard, Manchester, or to Warrington Arpley. In 1983 up to four trains a day would usually run carrying domestic coal destined for the depots at Ardwick, Buxton South, Chadderton, Guide Bridge, Liverpool Edge Hill, Rawtenstall, Southport and Stockport, as well as industrial coal for the Corn Products Co. in Trafford Park. On May 18 1983 Class 37 No. 37104 passes Manchester Victoria East signalbox with 8M15, the 10.15 SX Healey Mills to Warrington Arpley. Routed via the Calder Valley line, this freight had already called at Middleton Junction to detach a raft of loaded 21-ton hoppers for Chadderton coal depot, while its remaining 16 wagons included more hoppers loaded with coal for Liverpool and Southport as well as two Plate wagons en route to British Steel's Atherton Quay ironworks in Warrington.

By the early 1980s a large number of 21-ton Mineral wagons, coded MDO or MDV and initially built to carry industrial and power station coal, had been reallocated to domestic coal traffic and four MDVs were immediately behind Class 33 No. 33112 as it headed south near Warminster on October 20, 1980 with 6092, the 16.15 MO Severn Tunnel Junction to Eastleigh wagonload service. The MDVs were heading for the coal depot at Southampton Dibles Wharf, while also in the train were eight covered coil wagons returning empty from British Leyland's Swindon Works to the Poole Harbour Commissioners' sidings at Hamworthy to collect another consignment of imported cold reduced coil. At the rear of the fully-fitted formation can be seen five liquid petroleum gas tank wagons running discharged from the Inco Europe nickel smelter at Clydach-on-Tawe to the Esso refinery at Fawley.

One of the most well-known freight in the West Country was the 'Clayliner' which ran daily between St Blazey and Stoke to convey ball clay and china clay for use by the Potteries' ceramics industry. On its return journey 6V53 would stop at Exeter Riverside yard to detach any empty open wagons that were destined for the clay dries at Marland or Meeth, before continuing on from Exeter as a mixed freight. Class 45 No. 45138 passes a throng of holiday-makers at Dawlish Warren in August 1976 with several sheeted opens, a Vanfit, and a Conflat loaded with a wooden container, marshalled among the empty clay opens. *(© Colour Rail)*

The coal depots at Penzance, Plymouth Friary, and St Austell were officially closed in May 1984, although traffic had already ceased a few months earlier following the start of the miners' strike. St Austell, which received around 10,000 tonnes of coal a year, was served by a local trip from St Blazey recorded arriving back at Par behind Class 37 No. 37274 on May 6 1981. The Class 37 will reverse its short train around the curve into St Blazey yard, from where the two empty MDOs and the empty MCO and MCV will continue their journey back to the South Wales coalfield later that evening as part 8C58, the 20.50 SX to Severn Tunnel Junction.

The long-distance china clay traffic from the West Country was gradually switched to air-braked wagons during the early-1980s, but other freight in the area continued to be moved via the vacuum-braked network and on March 23, 1982 Class 45 No. 45122 was recorded at Aller Junction with 7B18, the 03.45 MX Severn Tunnel Junction to Plymouth Friary. Included in the train are two sheeted Pipe wagons loaded with military supplies for Devonport Dockyard, three empty Presflos en route from Barnstaple to Plymstock Cement Works, two Tube wagons in departmental traffic, while at the rear are two 16-ton Minerals for Plymouth Friary. By this date unfitted wagons had been banned west of Exeter and consequently, with the train being continuously braked, there was no requirement for a Brake Van.

By 1983 wagonload freight services were in a state of flux as revenue traffic was either transferred to the air-braked Speedlink network or else switched to road. Although booked as a 'Class 6' fully-fitted working the 13.50 SX Manchester Ashburys to Warrington Arpley would often run as a partially-fitted 'Class 8' to accommodate both vacuum and air-braked stock and Class 37 No. 37140 is pictured approaching Stockport with 8F45 from Ashburys on May 30, 1983. Immediately behind the locomotive is a vacuum-braked two-axle Class B tank, returning empty from Buxton TMD to Shell's Stanlow refinery, while also in the formation are three vacuum-braked Grampus, a Presflo and a Single Jib Crane along with its attendant Plate wagons and Mess Van, a modified ex-GWR 'Toad'. Towards the rear of the train, ahead of the Brake Van, are three air-brake wagons running unfitted; a bogie VTG ferry van, two-axle ferry van, and a telescopic hooded VTG coil van which was loaded with steel billets on their way to a customer in Italy. The billets had been rolled at GKN's Brymbo steelworks, near Wrexham, but as GKN's private sidings could not accept bogie wagons they had been roaded to Manchester Ardwick West freight depot to be loaded on to rail. However, within a year the billet movement had ceased; all traction gas oil traffic had been switched to air-braked tanks and the vacuum-braked BR Presflos had been withdrawn, while the transfer of a number of air-braked bogie bolster and open wagons to the Civil Engineers had begun the modernisation of the departmental fleet.

In August 1982 the old British Rail-owned 13-ton capacity five plank wooden open wagons used for long-distance china clay traffic were withdrawn and replaced by a fleet of 35 new bogie covered hoppers hired by English China Clays from the wagon leasing company Tiger Rail. They were known to rail staff and enthusiasts alike as 'Clay Tigers' and Class 47 No. 47089 had at least eight of the new wagons in tow as it headed 6B39, the 05.50 MSX Speedlink from Severn Tunnel Junction to Drinnick Mill, past Aller Junction on May 17, 1983. The train also included a bogie curtain-hooded van heading to Cornwall to be loaded with bagged china clay for the continent.

LEFT: The Procter & Gamble liveried PBAs and PCAs were confined to the Whitehaven to West Thurrock circuit but in 1984 a new batch of sodium tripolyphosphate PCAs was introduced to replace them. Subsequently two of the earlier wagons, PBA No. PR11300 and PCA No. PR10011, were sent to Ardwick West FD in Manchester to assess their suitability for carrying starch, being recorded there in February 1985. The trial was a success and eight of the PBAs were then leased by the Corn Products Co. for starch traffic from Manchester to several paper mills in Scotland.

Another working that might run as either an air or vacuum-braked service was 7P36, the 06.42 MSX Warrington Walton Old Junction to Carlisle via Workington. This served customers along the Cumbrian coast and is seen arriving at Sellafield behind a Class 40 on March 12, 1981 when formed entirely of air-braked stock; the inclusion of the Brake Van being due to the presence of loaded nuclear flask wagons in the train. The Class 40 is about to draw forward into the BNFL reprocessing plant sidings (which are behind the photographer) where the last nine vehicles: the six nuclear flask wagons, together with the pair of two-axle Swiss ferry tanks which were loaded with nitric acid used in the reprocessing of irradiated nuclear fuel, and the Brake Van will be detached. The Swiss tanks were on temporary hire to UKF Fertilisers and had originated at their chemical plant at Ince & Elton. Also in the train are three loaded caustic soda tanks bound for British Sidac at Wigton, and a VDA and three empty powder wagons all destined to Whitehaven's Preston Street goods yard. The powder wagons, two Procor bogie PBAs and one Procor two-axle PCA, were from a pool of 20 wagons then in use carrying sodium tripolyphosphate from the Albright & Wilson chemical plant at Whitehaven to Procter & Gamble's detergent factory at West Thurrock.

Across the length and breadth of the country more than 400 coal depots continued to be rail-served in 1980, although of those just 50 were handling more than 75% of the traffic and a programme to close many of the smaller under-utilised depots was already underway. On April 4, 1980 Class 73 No. 73107 nears Fleet with 6L76, the 12.34 SX Basingstoke Yard to Farnborough, its lightweight load comprising one 21-ton Mineral and one 16-ton Mineral loaded with phurnacite from Abercwmboi.

gton Olympia ⇌ InterCity

Some freight flows that had previously been moved in vacuum-braked block trains were transferred to the Speedlink network, including the movement of silica sand from British Industrial Sand's Holmethorpe Sidings at Redhill to the Joseph Crosfield & Sons soap and chemical works at Warrington. Instead of being delivered in a weekly train of 24-ton BR vacuum-braked hoppers, the sand would now arrive at Warrington two or three days a week loaded in four or five 37-tonne privately-owned air-braked hopper wagons. Class 33 No. 33004 heads through Kensington Olympia with 6M88, the 13.12 SX Crawley to Willesden Speedlink, on September 21, 1987 formed of five PGAs en route from Redhill to Warrington, along with an OBA and two bogie VTG ferry vans from the Dor-to-Dor distribution depot at Crawley.

As a result of the economic downturn of the early-1980s, which saw a significant decline in steel traffic, more than 250 air-braked Bogie Bolsters were reallocated to the departmental fleet in 1983. Recoded from BDA to YAA, with the Fishkind name 'BRILL', they were then used to carry both new and second-hand rail, YAA No. 950072 being recorded when loaded with used rail at Warrington Arpley in April 1985.

From the mid-1960s most petroleum products were conveyed by the trainload but the movement of traction gas oil to diesel depots and refuelling points remained a wagonload traffic right through the Speedlink era. Most locomotive depots had only limited storage for diesel and so relied upon regular deliveries of two or three tank wagons at a time, while some flows of both bitumen and liquid petroleum gas were also insufficient to warrant block train operation. On September 29, 1987 Class 33 No. 33010 passes Langstone Rock, immediately to the east of Dawlish, on the famous sea wall, with 6M17, the 12.10 Plymouth Tavistock Junction to Bescot Speedlink. The mixed formation included a VGA, three discharged LPG tanks returning from Shell's Plymouth Cattewater LPG terminal to BP's Grangemouth refinery, two Esso Class A tanks en route from Plymouth Laira TMD to Fawley, and three empty bitumen tanks also heading back to Fawley from the Esso depot at Plymouth Cattewater Harbour. The interesting train also includes two OBAs, modified for bogie/wheelset traffic by the removal of their sides, that were running from Plymouth Laira to BREL Crewe Works.

Until its closure in 1987 Severn Tunnel Junction acted as a major Speedlink hub for both South Wales and the West Country. In addition to up to two dozen trips, it was also the originating point for daily trunk services to other hub yards at Bescot, Doncaster, Dover, Mossend, Tees, Warrington and Whitemoor and Class 47 No. 47049 is pictured in September 1986 shortly after departure from Severn Tunnel Junction Down Yard with 6S75, the 12.55 Speedlink to Mossend. The train is comprised of a single FPA container wagon and two HEA coal hoppers, which were all loaded with domestic coal for depots in Scotland, along with a VTG ferry-fitted sliding-hood wagon followed by a raft of 10 VEAs in military traffic with an empty VAA at the rear acting as a barrier wagon. The transport of ammunition and explosives on behalf of the MoD was a common sight on this working, with regular movements between the Royal Ordnance Factories at Glascoed and Bishopton and military bases in the south west of England, South Wales and Scotland. *(© Trevor Mann collection)*

The development of the Speedlink network also resulted in rail regaining a significant share of domestic grain traffic, which by autumn 1986 amounted to more than 800,000 tonnes per annum. Most of this traffic was carried by a fleet of more than 100 59-tonne capacity 'Grainflow' Polybulk wagons hired from Traffic Service Ltd. which could be seen working from numerous loading points across East Anglia to distilleries in Scotland and flour mills at Birkenhead and Carlisle. Coded PIA No. 33 70 9280 067-7 awaits unloading outside the Spillers Homepride mill at Birkenhead in April 1987.

Illustrating the diversity of the traffic conveyed by wagonload services is this view of the same 6S75, 12.55 Speedlink working to Mossend, seen leaving Severn Tunnel Junction a year earlier on September 27, 1985 behind Class 25 No. 25279. On this occasion the consist included a raft of six bogie UKF fertiliser vans, which were returning from the West of England Farmers' siding at Melksham, Wiltshire, to the UKF chemical plant at Ince & Elton, as well as several empty Shell bitumen tanks on their way back to Stanlow from the King's Asphalt terminal at Exeter City Basin. Towards the rear of the train were a single LPG tank, two recently repainted bogie Class A petroleum tanks and a handful of HEAs carrying domestic coal. *(© Trevor Mann collection)*

Although it survived the demise of Speedlink, the light fittings traffic from Bodmin ceased in 1992 but in 1996 forwardings to Leith and Warrington returned to rail via Transrail's 'Enterprise' wagonload service. Birmingham Lawley Street was added to the list of destinations in 1998 but the workings from Bodmin, which involved the vans being tripped between Bodmin and Bodmin Parkway by the Bodmin & Wenford Railway, would ultimately prove to be uneconomic and the traffic finally came to an end in autumn 2001. Ten vans were allocated to Bodmin with VKAs Nos. 210490 and 210535 being spotted at the Fitzgerald Lighting's private siding in June 2001. The recoding to VKA indicated a former VGA that had been fitted with heavy-duty axles and journals.

Probably the greatest success of the air-braked wagonload network was in stemming the flow of existing traffic on to the roads, but a handful of new companies also began to use rail during the Speedlink era, such as Anchor Roof Tiles and Fitzgerald Lighting. Commencing in 1985 the Fitzgerald traffic, which comprised commercial light fittings, was initially railed from Truro to Gidea Park, Leith, and Warrington Dallam, while in 1989 a new private siding was built to serve the company's factory at Bodmin. From the outset the light fittings were carried in BR VGA sliding-wall vans and on August 8, 1988 Class 50 No. 50149 'Defiance', the only member of the class to be repainted in Railfreight livery, arrives at Par with a Plymouth to St Blazey trip consisting of two VGAs from Bodmin and a CDA, the latter en route from Lostwithiel to St Blazey C&W.

The advantage to Joseph Crosfield & Sons of receiving their sand 'little and often' was due to the cramped nature of the hopper unloading point within the depths of their Warrington works. However, when this was replaced by a more conveniently located facility in 1990 the traffic would be switched to road. One of the eight Standard Wagon-owned PGA two-axle hoppers allocated to the Crosfield sand traffic, PGA No. SRW 18520, is seen being unloaded at Warrington in October 1985. Indeed such was the tight radius of the track to reach the sand unloading point that the wagons were left by BR outside the Crosfield works entrance, from where a modified road tractor would be used to haul them singly over the hopper pit. Two of British Industrial Sand's own wagons, Nos. BIS 7955 and BIS 7957, await entry to the site in August 1989. The BIS hopper wagons had originally been built with hinged top covers for the carriage of dry sand from Middleton Towers to the glassworks at Barnby Dunn and Monk Bretton

By May 1984 all wagonload freight to the Cumbrian Coast and Furness lines was being carried in air-braked wagons. The southbound Speedlink services included 7F16, the 17.30 SX Carnforth to Warrington Arpley seen heading through Lancaster on July 16, 1984. Immediately behind Class 25 No. 25212 is a 29-tonne capacity VGA, a van-type first introduced by BR in 1982, which had been collected from the Boddy Transport & Storage depot at Carnforth after delivering a load of bagged china clay from Cornwall. Altogether more unusual was the third wagon in the train; this being the MoD's unique 80.5-tonne glw Nuclear Flask Transporter, No. MODA 95781, which was on its way back empty to Rolls Royce at Derby, having earlier in the month made one of its rare mainline forays to deliver a new nuclear submarine core to the Vickers Shipyard at Barrow-in-Furness. The consist also includes a loaded Plate wagon, several empty 45-tonne glw tank wagons returning from Barrow TMD to Stanlow refinery, and a number of Bogie Bolsters, and accompanying Runner wagons, which had recently been transferred to the Civil Engineers fleet. *(© Trevor Mann collection)*

Following the demise of Severn Tunnel Junction yard a smaller wagonload hub was established on the outskirts of Bristol at Stoke Gifford, although with the announcement of Speedlink's forthcoming closure its traffic soon began to decline as customers began switching their goods to road. Class 90 No. 90030 heads 6V93, the 07.30 SX Mossend to Stoke Gifford Speedlink, at Warrington Bank Quay on May 10, 1991 with only empty china clay and loaded timber wagons in the consist.

With the decline in wagonload traffic many freight facilities closed while others took on a very neglected appearance. Trafford Park West Sidings had once been a thriving exchange point with the Manchester Ship Canal Railway, who would forward wagons to numerous private sidings situated on the Barton Dock branch and within the Trafford Park industrial estate, but by June 1992 only a handful of wagons were present among the weeds, awaiting delivery to either Castle Steel Services or Norton Metals.

Elsewhere facilities underwent major rationalisation and at Tees Yard, near Middlesbrough, only the Up Departure Sidings and the Up Yard were being used by the late-1990s, with the rest of the once 130-siding-strong complex having been abandoned. However, a limited amount of marshalling continued to be undertaken and on May 28, 1998 Class 08 No. 08582 was recorded shunting a rake of Bogie Bolster wagons loaded with aluminium ingots. The ingots had arrived on a trip working from the Alcan smelter at Lynemouth and would go forward that night in a Tees Yard to Wolverhampton Steel Terminal service.

Privately owned vans have never been common in Britain, but between 1968 and 1975 some 90 bogie Palvans were built by the Gloucester Railway Carriage & Wagon Co., BREL Ashford, Procor and W.H. Davis, for the carriage of bagged fertiliser from the Shellstar (later UKF Fertilisers) chemical works at Ince & Elton in Cheshire to company depots and BR goods sidings across the country. Among the vans' unique features were an intermediate floor to fully utilise the wagons' 48-tonne capacity, and internal bulkheads and dunnage bags to prevent the load from moving in transit. The first batch of 30 had been built with curtain sides, but these proved to be difficult to secure and they were later replaced with four pairs of cupboard doors per side to match the rest of the fleet. PWA No. LS 7012, from the first batch, is seen in rebuilt condition at Warrington in April 1989. This batch also had four jacks, two at each end, by which the one-piece roof could be raised to ensure the four top compartments could be fully loaded, but by this date this feature had been disabled.

While Speedlink began to be rationalised in 1987, traffic levels in Scotland would remain buoyant until the network was closed in 1991. Class 20s Nos. 20185+20148 leave a busy Mossend yard with 7N67, the 10.02 SX to Stirling, on July 10, 1990. Included in the train are four BP Class A tanks, three Blue Circle Cement PCAs, and two OBAs and four OCAs, all destined for Grangemouth. The opens are carrying bricks from the Western Brick siding at Pinhoe, near Exeter, to JG Russell's Grangemouth depot, while towards the rear of the train are a number of loaded molasses tanks en route from the United Molasses siding at Greenock to the distillers' (yeast) plant at Menstrie. Other wagons in the packed yard include OTAs loaded with round timber, china clay slurry tanks, alumina powder PCAs, bogie bolsters loaded with steel pipes, two Cargowaggon 'Hold-All' covered vans in Norsk Hydro fertiliser traffic and a line of HEAs loaded with fragmented scrap. (© John Dedman)

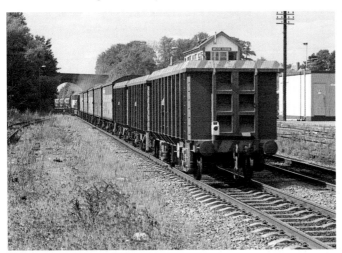

The end of Speedlink did not bring down the curtain on wagonload freight since Railfreight Distribution introduced its 'Connectrail' trains to handle goods arriving at Dover on the train ferry from Dunkirk to Dover, while the metals sector continued to run a handful of inter-yard workings handling traffic for more than one customer. Class 56 014 heads through Melton Mowbray with an empty Cargowaggon flat from Whittlesea, five empty BR vans from Metal Box at Wisbech, and three loaded POA scrap opens from Mayer Newman at Snailwell, forming 6V63, the 11.18 March to Cardiff and Margam, on September 20, 1991.

Despite its rationalisation, Tees Yard would retain a requirement for Class 08 shunting locomotives well into the 21st Century. In a busy scene recorded on March 13, 2005 No. 08813 is seen propelling a British Steel Teesside PGA, a British Steel Glasgow PAA and a BMA, towards the photographer; all three wagons being destined for attention at Thornaby Wagon Shop, as in the background a Class 60, running light engine from Lackenby to Thornaby TMD, has had to wait while an unidentified Class 08 in EWS livery shunts a long rake of empty BDAs into the old Up Yard.

Another metals sector train introduced to replace Speedlink was a daily working between Cardiff and Manchester. This carried steel rod and bar destined for the Castle Services siding at Trafford Park, as well as empty steel scrap opens for Norton's scrapyard also located within the Trafford Park industrial estate. In addition, the train often included wagons loaded with tinplate coil which were en route from BSC's Trostre Works to the Metal Box factory at Westhoughton. Class 37 No. 37906 rounds the sharp curve at the now-closed Miles Platting station with 6H65, the 12.40 return trip from Westhoughton, on April 26, 1991. Once back at Trafford Park West Sidings the Class 37 will add these wagons to any empties from Castle Services and loaded scrap from Norton's before heading back to South Wales.

Class 90 No. 90128 *'Vrachtverbinding'* barrels north through Carstairs with 6S70, the 03.40 MSX Crewe Basford Hall to Glasgow Deanside, on May 23, 1993. This train connected with an overnight Dover to Crewe service, but in addition to conveying traffic from the continent it also included vanloads of beer from the Guinness brewery at Park Royal heading for the Deanside Transit depot at Glasgow Shieldhall.

Train consist for 6S70 Crewe Basford Hall to Glasgow Deanside on May 23, 1993. In addition to the three IZA Twin-Vans carrying beer to Deanside, the consist included a Tiphook TIA powder wagon loaded with cationic starch from the continent for Aberdeen, as well as two empty Cargowaggon two-axle vans, an empty bogie ferry van and an empty Cargowaggon flat.

LEFT: In the immediate aftermath of the Speedlink closure, and until Railfreight Distribution's 'Connectrail' operation had become established, some European traffic hitched a ride on any convenient freight. A Class 37 heads east through Manchester Victoria in August 1991 with a Warrington Arpley to Castleton departmental working, the three bogie VTG ferry vans in the consist being loaded with cases of wine and ultimately destined for Manchester International Freight Terminal.

Aside from a handful of Class 90s Railfreight Distribution was reliant upon its fleet of ageing Class 47s to haul 'Connectrail' services and following the opening of the Channel Tunnel in 1994 double heading became the norm on trains running to and from Dollands Moor. Class 47s Nos. 47395 and 47222 negotiate Factory Junction, Wandsworth Road, with a long train of Cargowaggon vans forming a Wembley to Dollands Moor working in August 1995.

When it acquired the three Trainload Freight companies, EWS also inherited the handful of wagonload freights introduced by Transrail in 1994 under the 'Enterprise' brand and, at least for a few years, the new owners sought to increase the scope of such workings, integrating them with the erstwhile 'Connectrail' European services which they had also taken over. Soon a scaled down version of Speedlink had developed and Class 56 No. 56090 was recorded at Carlisle on May 1, 1998 with 6M27, the 14.48 SX Mossend to Bescot 'Enterprise'. As well as two twin-vans loaded with bottled whisky for the continent, the train included a short raft of sheeted PGA hoppers en route from Dalry to Middlewich.

In 2001 the Middlewich-Dalry salt traffic would be replaced by deliveries of hydrochloric acid from the Albion Inorganics chemical works at Sandbach. On April 22, 2005 Class 67 No. 67014, working 6F17, the 09.15 MWFO Sandbach to Warrington Arpley, hurries three loaded hydrochloric acid tanks through Acton Bridge on the first leg of their journey to Dalry.

Other than for departmental service the only other mixed freight working to be seen today are those moving wagons to and from repair. On April 17, 2019 Class 66 No. 66034 heads the 14.05 WO Warrington Arpley to Bescot Down Side south past Crewe Basford Hall Junction, its train comprising a WIA five-set fully-enclosed car carrier, three empty FQA bogie container flats, and a single HRA bogie aggregate hopper recently rebuilt from a HTA coal hopper at the Axiom Rail's Stoke-on-Trent works.

Foreign-registered ferry tank wagons had become something of a rarity by 2002, although the occasional one would still transit the Channel Tunnel. Photographed at Warrington in February 2002, ICA No. 33 87 7990 001-2 was one of three specially equipped 80-tonne glw, 55-tonne capacity, Locatransports tanks then in use carrying liquid sugar from France to the Roche plant at Dalry. In addition to its heavily lagged tank barrel, the wagon was fitted with an on-board heating unit, just discernible at the far end of the vehicle.

During its first decade EWS expanded the 'Enterprise' wagonload service to most parts of the country and on September 23, 2003 Class 66 No. 66085 was recorded at Cardiff heading 6B03, the 09.18 Swansea Burrows Sidings to Newport Alexandra Dock Junction. This lengthy train, which had called at Margam yard, included a single FPA coal container wagon, a long raft of ferry vans, several BYA steel coil carriers, plus three empty Esso 45-tonne tanks which were en route from Margam TMD to Fawley.

With the integration of freight service by EWS, the 'Enterprise' trains also began to handle Channel Tunnel traffic and Class 92 No. 92041 'Vaughan Williams' has entirely continental traffic in tow as it passes Hanstead with 6S75, the 10.42 SX Wembley to Mossend on April 24, 2002. In the consist are an IFA Euro-Twin loaded with Spedition Hammelmann tanktainers, which was en route from France to Scotland, an empty STVA car carrier returning to Washwood Heath, a bogie Simotra tank loaded with liquid sugar for the Roche pharmaceutical works at Dalry, and several bogie ferry vans. (©David Hayes)

Salt traffic from Middlewich to Dalry commenced in 1982, when Roche Products installed a rail siding at its Ayrshire pharmaceutical plant, and it would outlive the end of Speedlink, firstly as part of a multi-chemical contract service which also conveyed tank wagons of acetone and caustic soda to Dalry, and later via the Enterprise service operated by Transrail and EWS. A pool of 25 Procor 51-tonne glw salt hoppers was available for the traffic; PR 8268 and PR 8909 being recorded awaiting collection at the British Salt works in Middlewich on February 28, 1997.

The Spedition Hammelmann tanktainers carried nutriose, a water-soluble dextrin powder with a high dietary fibre content used in a variety of food products and fibre supplements, from the Roquette works at Lestrem, near Béthune in northern France, to the Roche Products plant at Dalry in Ayrshire. IFA Euro-Twin No. 31 87 4908 114-3 was loaded with four of the specialist tanktainers when photographed at Warrington Arpley in June 2001.

RIGHT: In 2007 EWS was sold to Deutsche Bahn AG (DB) but with other railfreight operators such as Freightliner and GBRf beginning to win some of its valuable bulk flows, the new owners concentrated their resources on improving trainload services and the wagonload business was allowed to slowly fade away. One freight flow that lasted until 2012 was the movement of granulated limestone from Redland's Dowlow quarry at Hindlow, south of Buxton, to the PD Stirling terminal at Mossend and on August 9, 2007 Class 67 No. 67019 leaves Peak Forest Holding Sidings with a late-running 6F67, the 10.16 Dowlow to Warrington Arpley 'Enterprise' trip. In addition to the first four covered hoppers which were all from Dowlow, the train includes three empty HOA bogie hoppers en route from the Cemex sidings at Peak Forest to Warrington for maintenance.

CHAPTER 2

Goods Depots and Private Sidings

In 1977 BR still provided cranage facilities for handling steel and other heavy loads at more than 80 freight depots, although these were rather thinly spread in some parts of the country. One area that was still relatively well-served was the old county of Lancashire, where individual items weighing up to 11 tons could be handled at Bolton, Carlisle London Rd, Heysham, Liverpool Canada Dock, Manchester Ardwick, Warrington Central and Wigan North Western. However, changes in wagonload operations were mirrored by a decline in the number of BR freight depots with such facilities and Bolton, Warrington Central and Wigan would all close during the 1980s. The Cheshire Lines Committee goods warehouse at Warrington Central survived until 1982, and in this April 1977 view two BR Vanfits and a pair of new VTG bogie ferry vans await unloading. Ferry vans were then a common sight at the depot, arriving with cases of wine from the continent.

By the late-1980s many BR freight depots, if not already closed, had been downgraded to public delivery sidings. These were usually devoid of any storage capability with wagon loading and unloading undertaken by a local road haulier on behalf of the consignee or consignor. On March 30, 1989 a Danzas ferry van is unloaded at Carlisle London Road after arriving with paperboard from the continent.

At Bolton the old Lancashire & Yorkshire warehouse remained open until the end of August 1984, with vanloads of bagged china clay from Cornwall and boxed dyestuffs from the continent some of the last commodities to be handled. The final forklift of bagged china clay from Par is unloaded from VAA No. 200049 at Bolton on August 20, 1984. It is believed this was the last van to arrive at the depot, which would be closed to all rail traffic the following week.

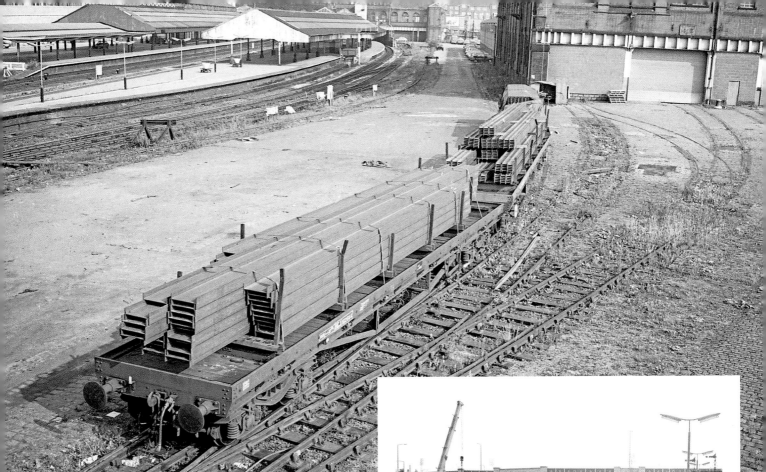

ABOVE AND RIGHT: Also among the last traffics to be seen at Bolton Trinity Street were occasional consignments of steel plate or section from Scunthorpe, which would arrive loaded on to Bogie Bolster D or Trestle wagons. Three BDAs carrying steel section await unloading at Bolton on July 30, 1984.

RIGHT: During the 1980s the Potter Group opened rail-served distribution depots at Ely and Selby, and these were followed in 2001 by a third depot at Knowsley. Each depot handled a range of commodities, although the one at Knowsley concentrated primarily on receiving imported paper from Scandinavia, and one of Potter's own Class 08s No. 08202 is pictured shunting ferry vans at Knowsley alongside Loadhaul liveried Class 56 No. 56112 in July 2012. A few years later the Potter Group sold its warehousing and transport operations and all rail traffic at its terminals then ceased, but since 2016 the Knowsley site has been brought back into use by the Merseyside Recycling & Waste Authority as the loading point for a rail-carried flow of domestic refuse to Wilton.

The small goods yard at Blackburn Bolton Road was taken over by PG Fogarty in 1980 primarily as a distribution depot for steel, although it did also receive vanloads of chipboard and wine from the continent and tank wagons of chalk slurry from Aberdeen, which was destined for the local wallpaper mills. Class 60 No. 60078 propels two IHA Tiphook (ex-VTG) ferry-fitted sliding-hood wagons into the depot on May 1, 1998. These wagons, which had first been introduced in 1979, were used to deliver coiled steel from both the Continent and the British Steel works at Lackenby and Port Talbot. Unfortunately many small privately operated distribution depots such as those at Blackburn and Wakefield ceased to use rail when the 'Enterprise' wagonload service was run down.

Until 1984 the goods yard at Wakefield Kirkgate handled trainloads of containerised coke from the Derwenthaugh coking plant, near Newcastle-upon-Tyne. Subsequently the site was redeveloped by Cobra Railfreight and a 5,000 sq m covered warehouse constructed so that wagons of moisture-sensitive cold reduced coil ('bright steel') from British Steel's Llanwern and Port Talbot works could be unloaded under cover. The depot also handled other steel flows including rod coil from Cardiff and Sheerness and billet from Germany. Two Cargowaggon flats wait to be unloaded at Wakefield on January 15, 2000.

Many regular freight customers, such as the Rank Hovis McDougall flour mill at Birkenhead, had their own private sidings. Two-axle bulk grain vans, loaded with wheat from Byford Grain at Chettisham, are pictured outside the RHM Ocean Mill at Birkenhead Docks in May 1985.

In 2002 the line from Kingsbury Branch Junction, that had once reached the closed Baddesley Colliery, was relaid to serve a new TNT/Volkswagen distribution depot and adjacent container terminal at Birch Coppice. Imported automotive components, carried in Cargowaggon twin-vans, were worked to Birch Coppice by a daily trip from Bescot and Class 37 No. 37896 is seen passing Kingsbury with the return working on September 11.

LEFT: Following the closure and demolition of the British Oxygen Co. plant at Widnes, the site retained its rail connection and in 1998 it was brought back into use by O'Connor's Transport and AHC Warehousing as a general freight terminal. Most of the traffic handled at Widnes was carried in containers, but for a couple of years the terminal was also used as a loading point for ferry tank wagons in arcton traffic to the continent, this arriving by road tanker over the Silver Jubilee Bridge from ICI's nearby works at Runcorn. However, when additional intermodal services to Widnes were introduced in 2008 the transshipment arrangement was moved from Widnes to Warrington Dallam freight depot. Bogie VTG tank No. 33 80 7894 023-0 awaits loading at Widnes Foundry Lane in January 2006.

At Birch Coppice a Unimog road-rail vehicle No. 9210 was used to shunt the auto parts vans into the TNT Logistics warehouse, just in view to the left, until that traffic was switched to road in 2007, but fortunately container traffic continues and in 2019 there were daily workings from both Felixstowe and Southampton Maritime.

ABOVE AND RIGHT: The Bowaters paper mill at Sittingbourne had an extensive narrow gauge rail system within the works, while standard gauge wagons delivering clay slurry were dealt with at a two-road shed built alongside the Rochester to Canterbury line. In April 1995 the unloading shed was handling wagons carrying china clay slurry from Burngullow and chalk slurry from both Aberdeen and Quidhampton.

ABOVE AND LEFT: The previous closure of numerous wayside sidings and small freight depots, coupled with the exorbitant cost of reinstating rail connections, has meant that in recent years attracting short-term flows has proved difficult. Fortunately the sidings at Ribblehead, on the Settle & Carlisle line, have remained in place and between 2010 and 2014 were used as a loading point for locally grown timber which was then despatched to the Kronospan board mill at Chirk. Colas Rail's Class 66 No. 66843 (ex-DRS 66408) waits for its train to be loaded at Ribblehead in August 2011.

Today most freight traffic is handled at company private sidings or large container terminals, but a handful of small facilities, often no more than a short siding, remain in use as transfer points for nuclear flask traffic on its way to Sellafield. FNA No. 550012 is pictured inside the secure compound at Bridgwater awaiting the arrival of the next loaded flask by road from Hinckley Point power station in June 2001.

The usefulness of the sidings at Ribblehead again came to the fore a few years later when they began being used to load stone from the nearby Ingleton Quarry. On a very wet July morning in 2019 Class 66 No. 66769 prepares to leave Ribblehead with its loaded train of Ermewa and GBRf JNA wagons forming 6E53, the 09.53 departure for the Hanson asphalt depot at Leeds.

CHAPTER 3

In 1986 two IVAs were built for Cargowaggon by Duwag with their payload increased to 30t and this design was subsequently developed into the Twin-Van, a pair of two-axle vans permanently coupled which dispensed with conventional buffing gear at their inner ends bringing down the tare to give a combined payload of 62.5t. In all 200 Twin-vans, coded IZA, were built between 1986 and 1991 finding use in international traffic carrying chipboard, domestic appliances, mineral water and wines and spirits, while they were also used on several domestic freight flows, including beer from Park Royal, newsprint from Immingham, pet food from Glasgow Shieldhall and cider from Taunton. In 1999 GE Rail purchased a further 100 Twin-vans built by Waggon Union, these having a more rounded profile than previous IZAs which increased cubic capacity and their payload to 63t. Initially they were expected to carry automotive components between Germany and a BMW engine plant at Hams Hall, but when this traffic failed to materialise some were leased to UPM to carry paper between Irvine and Shotton. IZA No. 23 80 2929 250-1 from the final batch of Twin-vans and with a UPM logo on the door waits to leave Warrington en route from Caledonian Paper at Irvine to Shotton in August 2003.

A Variety of Vans – From Vanfits to Hold-Alls

As with all freight rolling stock the development of the covered van involved an increase in carrying capacity and a switch to air-braking, while by the 1980s bogie designs were becoming increasingly common. However, the decline of wagonload freight traffic in favour of more containerised handling has meant that vans are now an uncommon sight on Britain's railways.

LEFT: To complete outstanding orders, the years immediately following nationalisation saw BR build a number of 12t vans to the designs of the GWR, LMS and SR. Most numerous of these were the 1,000 LMS-design plywood-bodied sliding-door vans built to diagram 1/200 at Wolverton in 1949. Unsurprisingly they would be withdrawn from revenue service earlier than the BR standard vans, but two were among the dozen vans allocated to the carriage of timetables and other printed materials the short distance between the BRB Paper & Printing Stationary Stores, situated near the BREL Works at Crewe, and Crewe station. Here the wicker hampers of newly printed material would be transferred to parcels and passenger trains for distribution around the country. ZRV No. XDB751061, branded 'To Work Between/Crewe Station And/Crewe Stationary Stores', awaits unloading at Crewe station in August 1981. In this instance the 'XD' prefix to the wagon number signifies a vehicle belonging to the Stores Department.

For easier loading of palletised goods, BR experimented with several different body designs, the most successful being the Vanwide, with some 2,000 built at Wolverton between 1961 and 1963. Its most distinguishing feature was the pair of sliding-doors each side, which when opened gave a generous loading width of 9ft. The doors had steel-lined reinforced pockets situated at two different heights behind the steel locking bars and could be opened using the tines of a fork-lift, although carry capacity remained at 12 tons and the underframe was to the RCH standard dimensions of 17ft 6in over headstock with a 10ft wheelbase. The Vanwide proved to be a popular type with many customers, including Cadbury and Rowntree-Mackintosh, who both utilised them to carry their confectionery products to distribution depots across the country. Several years after use in Rowntrees traffic had ceased, VWV No. B783773 still retained its 'RETURN TO YORK' lettering when recorded at Swansea Burrows Sidings in August 1989.

Another van designed for palletised traffic was the Heinz Palvan, which at 20ft long, with a 12ft wheelbase, could carry 14 tons. Each side was formed of two pairs of cupboard-doors, the ends being heavily reinforced with T-beam uprights, and the interior divided into four sections by means of three vertical partitions. Inflatable dunnage bags to keep the pallets in place were also fitted and the vans were built to carry tinned foods such as baked beans and soups between the Heinz factories at Kitt Green, Wigan, and Harlesden, north London. However, the company soon switched its traffic to road and the vans were then reassigned to carry material for the MoD. The Heinz vans were fitted with a version of the LMS clasp brake with central V-hanger, short brake levers and auxiliary spring hangers, as seen in this view of VPV No. B782859 taken at Barry scrapyard when awaiting cutting up in August 1979. Also partially visible is No. B782402, one of 250 'Izal Palvans' built in 1960 to carry cleaning and hygiene products from Newton Chambers' new factory at Chapeltown, near Sheffield. These were 18ft 9in over headstocks with four sliding doors each side, but like the Heinz vans, use in their intended traffic proved to be short-lived and in the 1970s they could be found carrying Ford automotive components, Campbell's tinned soups and military stores. (©Don Farmborough/Trevor Mann collection)

The standard BR 12t Vanfit, of which more than 25,000 were built, married the GWR's wooden-bodied cupboard-door design with corrugated steel ends as adopted by the LMS and LNER. All were constructed on a steel underframe, 17ft 6in over headstocks with a 10ft wheelbase, and fitted with either RCH four-shoe vacuum brake gear or BR clasp brakes. Both planked and plywood-sided Vanfits were built and until the late-1970s they could still be found across the length and breadth of the rail network, carrying a wide variety of goods including bagged china clay from Par, bagged starch from Manchester, crated books from Dundee, fibreglass rolls from Panteg and sacks of malt from Wallingford. Vanfits were also still required in considerable numbers to move seasonal traffic such as bagged fertiliser, seed potatoes and sugar beet pulp nuts, a by-product from the sugar refining process used as an animal feed. However, as their use in revenue traffic declined a few Vanfits were transferred to the departmental fleet for the carriage of railway stores and equipment, although with only a 5ft ¼in door opening they were not ideal for handling larger items. VVV No. CDB776051 was one of two Vanfits allocated to BREL Swindon Works and when photographed at BREL Derby Litchurch Lane Works in August 1981 had recently arrived with a load of new hydraulic buffers. Note the chalked recoding to ZRV, reflecting its new status as a departmental wagon, while the 'CD' prefix to its number indicated a vehicle allocated to BREL. This diagram 1/213 all plywood-bodied Vanfit had been built at Faverdale Wagon Works, Darlington, in 1957.

Based on experimental long-wheelbase van No. B 787395 the first production batch of BR air-braked vans, initially coded COV AB and numbered 200000-324, was built at Ashford between 1969 and 1971. They had sides formed by two sliding-doors and were fitted with UIC double-link suspension. Painted in freight brown, the first 208 were subsequently coded VAB on TOPS with many having a yellow ABN (Air-Braked Network) circle on the side. Over the years these vans were to carry a myriad of commodities, including beer, breakfast cereals, commercial explosives, confectionery, fertiliser, mineral water, palletised jute, paper, preserves, rod coil and zinc ingots. They were also commonly used for military traffic, carrying everything from ammunition to tins of paint and varnish. When photographed at Warrington Arpley yard in May 1982 VAB No. 200019 was in commercial explosives traffic from the ICI/Nobel Explosives factory at Gathurst, near Wigan.

In 1982 British Rail switched to a sliding-wall design when Shildon Works built 251 two-axle vans for the Speedlink network. Coded VGA they were 42ft 1in over headstocks with a 29ft 6in wheelbase and had an impressive door opening of 20ft 8in by 7ft 2in, as illustrated by this view of No. 210548 loaded with mineral water at Warrington Dallam FD in May 1998. Fitted with Bruninghaus springs, these vans could carry 29 tonnes at 60mph and 24 tonnes at 75mph.

In contrast to the COV ABs the COV CDs, which would become VCAs on TOPS, were fitted with two central sliding-doors which gave a 16ft wide opening. Some 225, numbered 200325-549, were built at Ashford and Shildon between 1971 and 1974 and were intended to replace the Shocvans in tinplate traffic from South Wales to the numerous Metal Box factories around the country, the COV CD design enabling them to carry a higher load per square metre of floor to cope with the heavy tinplate packages. By the mid-1980s tinplate traffic had declined and many were transferred to the departmental fleet while a few were used to carry military explosives on behalf of the MoD. Only recently repainted, VCA No. 200364 glows in the early evening sun at Warrington Arpley yard in February 1987.

Italian State Railways owned a large fleet of two-axle vans of wooden construction and they were frequent visitors to Britain loaded with Italian imports including citrus fruits, furniture, shoes and wine. Another important traffic in the 1980s was domestic appliances, and when photographed at Dewsbury Railway Street freight depot ILB No. 21 83 2382 691-5 was loaded with washing machines. At 26-tonne capacity it was one of 400 vans built by Officine Flore in 1969 and measured 46ft long with a single sliding door.

The third design of BR air-braked van was the VDA of which 750 were built between 1975 and 1978. Of similar dimensions to BR's earlier air-braked vans, the underframe had a noticeably deeper frame between the wheels and the sides were formed of a combination of cupboard and sliding doors. A pair of central sliding doors gave an opening of 16ft 4in with cupboard doors either side, each of which provided an 8ft 2in opening. Large numbers were allocated to Rowntrees traffic to replace the Vanwides, but they could be found carrying a myriad of other wagonload commodities until the early 1990s. VDA No. 200681, repainted in the Railfreight dark grey and yellow livery introduced a couple of years earlier, is pictured at Mossend in July 1990. This was one of 10 VDAs then in Bulmers cider traffic from Hereford to Scotland.

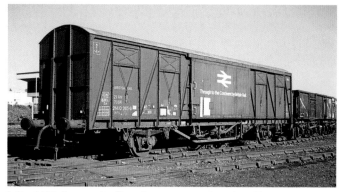

In the 1960s longer wheelbase ferry vans were introduced by many European railway administrations, including British Rail who owned 400 dual-braked 25-tonne capacity vans built between 1962 and 1964. They were 41ft 11in over headstocks with a single 13ft sliding door, and like many ferry vans were fitted with ventilators to facilitate the carriage of fresh fruit and vegetables. The BR ferry vans were coded VIX and No. 21 70 2140 265-5 was recorded at Northampton on October 21, 1979. By 1984 all the VIXs were out of ferry traffic, although many found further use as barrier wagons while others were subsequently transferred to the departmental fleet. *(©Don Farmborough/Trevor Mann collection)*

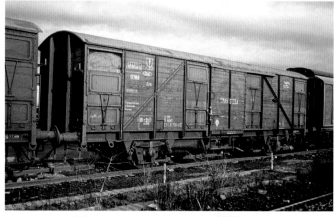

Most common of all the foreign-registered two-axle ferry vans were those belonging to the Spanish company Transfesa. These heavily ventilated vans were a common sight throughout Britain loaded with imported fruit and vegetables and ITX No. 24 71 2148 704-2 was loaded with onions when recorded at Ardwick West FD, Manchester, in February 1986.

Many small goods depots and private sidings which had opened in the Victorian era were inaccessible to larger vehicles and in consequence bogie vans had been an uncommon sight. However, this changed in 1977 when the German wagon leasing companies Cargowaggon and VTG introduced first 80t, and then 90t glw, bogie ferry vans for service between the continent and Britain. For their day they were real monsters, the 80t VTG vans being 62ft long while the Cargowaggon vans were even longer at 71ft 5in. Built by Link Hoffmann Busch, VTG owned 140 of these Type F1 vans, their sides consisting of three sliding doors and they could carry 55t, a huge increase on existing van designs. IPB 2180 0298 076-9 is pictured at Harwich loaded with bags of wafolin, a livestock feedstuff additive, in September 1977.

(©David Ratcliffe collection)

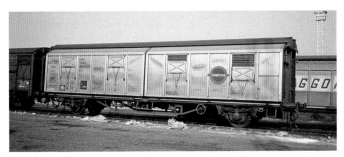

In 1983 Cargowaggon and Transfesa both introduced fleets of two-axle sliding wall ferry vans for cross-Channel service. Most of the Cargowaggon vans were initially allocated to automotive component traffics, some being leased to Ford for traffic between Dagenham and Halewood and others to Volkswagen to supply its spares depot at Wolverton, while the Transfesa vans carried perishables. More than 400 all-steel Transfesa vans would be built, all being fitted with four ventilators per side and having a capacity of 26 tonnes. ITX No. 24 71 2396 020-2 is pictured at Ardwick West in February 1985.

Largest of the bogie VTG ferry vans was the Type F3 which at more than 68ft in length could carry 63 tonnes. The type was first introduced into cross-Channel traffic in 1985 and IPA No. 83 70 2795 315-2 was recorded at Warrington Arpley on April 12, 1986.

For the 90-tonne glw ferry vans the design was modified with the sides formed from two sliding doors providing access to half the interior at a time. A handful of the Cargowaggon vans were painted in Perrier livery, which was an important cross-Channel traffic for several years. However, when recorded at Longport FD in April 1999, IPB No. 33 80 2797 702-8 had been transferred to the general ferry pool and was loaded with rod coil for the local Michelin tyre factory.

Cargowaggon also developed the 'Hold-All' of which 160 were built for general train ferry service by Waggon Union in 1987. Fitted with a two-piece telescopic hood, which when one half was opened slid up and over the other by means of a mechanical transmission, they were 19.52m long and could carry 63.5t. IWA No. 83 80 4741 159-3 was loaded with steel tubes destined for the Manchester International Freight Terminal when recorded at Trafford Park yard in November 1991.

CHAPTER 4

The Ministry of Defence, like its predecessors the Ministry of Supply and the War Department, has been an important freight customer making considerable use of the wagonload network to move supplies between its various installations across the country. Indeed some freight-only branch lines, like those between Andover and Ludgershall and Appleby and Warcop, were retained solely for military traffic. By the early 1980s military traffic was also the only freight to be seen on several other branch lines, such as the Plymouth to Gunnislake line which saw occasional workings to and from the Royal Navy depot at Ernesettle. Class 47 No. 47204 heads 6C39, the 09.30 St Blazey to Severn Tunnel Junction Speedlink through Bristol on June 20, 1984. This train called at Tavistock Junction yard, Plymouth, where on this occasion it had attached an MoD Warflat and Warwell both loaded with narrow gauge rolling stock from Ernesettle.

Military Manoeuvres

BR's decision to transfer its wagonload business to the air-braked network had posed a problem for the MoD, since the severe curvature of some of the sidings found inside its depots and ordnance factories meant that they could not accept BR's new long wheelbase AB vans and opens. Consequently between 1977 and 1984 some 50 Pipe wagons and 550 Vanwides were fitted with FAT 19 BR friction-link suspension and air-braked for continued use in military traffic. The modified Pipes were recoded ODA, No. 113013 being recorded at Warrington Walton Old Junction in August 1988, while the air-braked Vanwides became VEAs with No. 230039 photographed at Warrington Bank Quay when en route from Bishopton to Glascoed in April 1987.

Although much military traffic was entrusted to the wagonload network, occasionally special working would run on behalf of the Ministry of Defence. Class 86 No. 86005 is pictured at Warrington Bank Quay heading 6Z75, the 08.30 Carlisle Kingmoor to Marchwood, in May 1982. The consist included an empty OAA, marshalled immediately behind the locomotive as a barrier wagon, as well as a dozen VEAs all loaded with ammunition and explosives from Longtown Central Ordnance Depot, which was destined for shipment to the South Atlantic.

The Ministry of Defence has always had its own industrial locomotives for shunting within military depots, although their numbers began to decline during the 1980s. One location to retain its industrials was Ludgershall and on July 22, 1991 MOD No. 260, a 300 bhp Thomas Hill "Vanguard" 4wDH, works No. TH300V built 1982, shunts BR air-braked vans which had arrived earlier in the day loaded with medical supplies for the Defence Medical Equipment Unit.

The MoD also operated its own fleet of bogie Warflat and Warwell wagons which were used to carry vehicles and other large pieces of military equipment, although the routine use of these vehicles across the network has fallen away in recent years. Coded PFB Warflat No. MODA 95289, one of several recorded at Morpeth in September 1982, is loaded with a one-tonne '101' Landrover which were often used as artillery tractors for the 105mm light gun.

The Warwell was a Second World War design with 60 being refurbished in 1976 with new bogies, air-brakes and a through vacuum pipe. KWB No. MODA95537 is pictured at Ludgershall on July 22, 1991. The two bogie VTG vans in the background had arrived earlier that week from Germany with supplies for the Medical Equipment Unit.

By 1992 the VEAs had been withdrawn from main line use and the Army was making increasing use of containers to move its various stores around the country. On September 10, 1992 one of the Army's 335hp Thomas Hill 'Steelman' locomotives, No. 272 *'Royal Pioneer'*, works No. TH320V shunts a Tiphook bogie KFA at Bicester

The Speedlink era witnessed a considerable increase in the movement of imported mineral water and Cargowaggon Twin-Van, IZA No. 23 80 2794 005-1 was one of a handful specially repainted in Perrier livery, being recorded at Blackburn Freight Depot in June 1988.

Speedlink Raises a Glass

The carriage of both alcoholic and non-alcoholic beverages saw a marked increase during the 1980s, with companies like Grants of St James's, Perrier Vittel and Taunton Cider all being attracted to rail by the improved transit times that Speedlink offered. The cross-Channel flows included imports of bulk wine in tank wagons, via both the Dunkirk to Dover and Zeebrugge-Harwich train ferries, to bottling plants at Aylesbury, Guildford, Newhaven and Telford, while bottled wines and spirits arrived from the continent in both two-axle and bogie ferry vans en route to freight depots across the country.

The Dover-Dunkirk route also saw regular imports of Perrier water from Vergeze in southern France to the Isis Link depots at Ashford and Barking, the LCP terminal at Pensnett, Railstore at Gidea Park and United Transport in Cowley, while in 1990 trainloads of Volvic and Evian water also began arriving from the continent by rail, destined to the TP Dibden warehouse at Neasden. French, German and Italian state-owned two-axle ferry vans were a common sight in these movements until the early 1990s, when Cargowaggon and VTG ferry vans began carrying the lion's share of this traffic. Exports in this sector were dominated by the movement of bottled whisky from the blending and bottling plant at Glasgow, Kilmarnock, Leith and Perth, and this traffic formed a significant share of the backloads carried by continentally registered vans returning to Europe.

Domestic drinks traffic also expanded, and Bulmers was another well-known company to spot the advantages of Speedlink, despatching around six or seven van-loads of cider each day from Hereford to its customers in Scotland and the north of England. Forwarding of beer from the Guinness brewery at Park Royal in west London, a long-standing rail traffic that had been in steady decline since the early 1970s, also picked up once the 12-ton Vanfits previously used were replaced by a pool of air-braked vans, with the company using BR's Liverpool Spekeland Road and Tyneside Central Freight Depot and the private freight terminals operated by Deanside Transit at Glasgow Shieldhall, Selby Storage at Selby and Gower Chemicals at Swansea as regional distribution centres.

Other drinks traffic to originate on the Western Region included cider from both Taunton and Whimple and 'Steam Beer' from Truro, while Showerings of Shepton Mallet, producers of the light sparkling perry Babycham, also used rail, with its products being loaded on to rail at Bridgwater freight depot. Elsewhere, Speedlink also gained a foothold in the movement of soft drinks produced by Cadbury Schweppes, such as Lilt and Rose's Lime Juice, which were railed from the TWF Warehousing at Wolverton to Aberdeen, Glasgow and Leith, while Irn-Bru and Tizer, made by AG Barr in Cumbernauld, were railed from Glasgow Shieldhall to Rail Handling Services at Barking. Furthermore, the growing demand for bottled mineral water was not only met by increased imports, but the Speedlink network also began to handle the movement of Highland Spring Water from Perth to several destinations in England.

Following the demise of Speedlink in 1991 the import and export flows continued to be handled via the new Connectrail services, but much of the hard-won domestic drinks traffic was lost to road. Both Taunton Cider and Guinness would persevere with rail for a couple more years, but by 1993 their traffic had also been lost resulting in the closure of the private sidings at Norton Fitzwarren and Park Royal. In 1992 the newly introduced Glasgow to Cricklewood 'Charterail Piggyback' service included bottled water and soft drinks among its various loads, but the working quickly fell victim to the financial collapse of Charterail. However, in 1997 the revived 'Enterprise' wagonload service won a contract to transport Lovat Spring mineral water from Inverness in conventional two-axle air-braked vans to several destinations including Avonmouth, Blackburn, Ely, Gidea Park and Warrington Dallam, while VBAs and VGAs were also used to carry Ben Shaws mineral water from the Cobra Railfreight depot at Wakefield to Victa Rail at Hoo Junction.

In July 1999 EWS ran several trainloads of bottled water to Truro to cater to the needs of the increased numbers visiting Cornwall to witness the total eclipse, with this traffic being carried in both vans and 40ft containers loaded on to FAA wagons. EWS also regained some of the Guinness traffic with tanktainers of stout and lager being carried by the Wembley to Mossend 'Enterprise' service until the Park Royal brewery closed in 2005, while other containerised drinks flows have included imports of wine and spirits from Ipswich Dock to Widnes and from Tilbury to Bristol. The various Anglo-Scottish intermodal trains operated in recent years on behalf of Asda, Malcolm and Tesco, have also carried an assortment of bottled drinks.

Class 08 No. 08532 heads through Warrington Bank Quay with the local trip from Warrington Dallam FD to Warrington Arpley yard in April 1984. Its train consists of two VDAs, which had arrived at Dallam freight depot earlier in the week with cases of Babycham from Bridgwater, and a three-door VTG bogie ferry van which was returning empty to the continent after having delivered a consignment of French wine to Dallam.

Two of the sidings in the Wellington goods depot were dedicated to unloading the wine tanks and in the early-1980s Telford Bottling received around a dozen such 57-tonne capacity tank wagons each week.

In July 1985 a pair of Class 20s have charge of 6T41, the 08.30 Bescot to Wellington Speedlink trip, seen at Wolverhampton High Level station in July 1985. This working regularly included wine tanks which had arrived in Britain through Harwich and were en route to the Telford Bottling sidings at Wellington.

Ermefer wine tank 34 87 7890 518-5 is seen at the Telford Bottling sidings at Wellington after arriving from France loaded with Cinzano in July 1985. Towards the end of the decade demand for Cinzano vermouths diminished considerably and this traffic ceased.

A pair of three-door VTG vans carrying cases of wine for Grants of St James's are unloaded at Warrington Dallam in April 1986.

By the 1990s Guinness was using smaller casks, as pictured in this view of Cargowaggon Twin-van No. 23 80 2793 070-6 being unloaded at Otis Europe's Ordsall Lane freight terminal in May 1992. Guinness had switched its north west rail destination from Liverpool Spekeland Road to Ordsall Lane, Salford in 1989.

Traffic from the Guinness Park Royal brewery increased considerably once the standard 12t Vanfits, which could hold only 117 casks, were replaced by BR air-braked vans which were able to accommodate 330. With Draught Guinness stickers on its sides for publicity purposes, COV AB No. 200043 is seen at Park Royal in 1980. *(©Roger Silsbury collection)*

French-registered Euro-Twin IFA No. 33 87 4908 013-5 was loaded with containers of Guinness and Harp Irish Lager from Park Royal when spotted heading north at Rugby in the consist of 6S77, the 17.11 Wembley – Mossend 'Enterprise' service, on May 14, 2002.

The success of Speedlink encouraged both Bulmers of Hereford and Taunton Cider at Norton Fitzwarren to despatch much of their product destined to customers in Scotland and the north of England by rail. Most of this traffic was carried in BR air-braked vans, but in addition two bogie Cargowaggon vans repainted in their livery were leased by Taunton Cider. IPB No. 83 80 2797 687-9 is pictured at Warrington Arpley when returning with empty bottles from the Isis Link depot at Law Junction to Norton Fitzwarren in May 1987.

Following the demise of Speedlink the Guinness traffic from Park Royal to Ordsall Lane would remain on rail for a further three years, conveyed by a new daily block train. This company working, which could load up to eight Cargowaggon IZA 'Twin-vans', also called at Crewe Basford Hall to detach vans destined for Glasgow Shieldhall, these then continuing their journey north on 6S70, the Crewe to Glasgow 'Connectrail' service which ran primarily to convey cross-Channel freight. Class 47 No. 47351 heads 6V15, the 10.14 Ordsall Lane to Park Royal through Manchester Victoria on July 10, 1992.

Mineral water was a major rail import and arrived not only in VTG and Cargowaggon vans, but also in Transfesa bogie ferry vans. Built by Waggon Union in 1987, PIB No. 83 70 2795 360-8 was spotted at Warrington Dallam FD in October 1989.

Following privatisation, bottles of both carbonated and still Lovat Spring mineral water were railed in former BR air-braked vans, many now repainted in EWS livery, from Inverness to several destinations in England. VBA No. 200250 awaits unloading at Warrington Dallam FD in May 1998.

CHAPTER 6

Intermodal Traffic

From its earliest days Freightliner's own containers were concentrated on domestic and Anglo-Irish services and the preponderance of them is evident in this view of Class 87 No. 87019 heading down the WCML near Rugby with 4D62, the daily 16.05 Willesden to Holyhead Freightliner, in April 1975. Also notable is the large number of 10ft containers still in use at this date.

The carriage of containers by rail dates back to the 19th Century, but prior to the development of the Freightliner network in the 1960s the earlier containers had been built of wood, of three or four tonnes capacity, and carried on short-wheelbase wagons usually in wagonload services. Despite their small size they still delivered some of the inherent advantages of containerised transport – reduced load handling and the convenience of door-to-door delivery – but requiring a traditional jib crane to lift them on and off the wagon, and chains to hold them in place during transit, their operation was cumbersome and time-consuming.

BR had introduced revised methods of securing traditional containers with its Anglo-Scottish 'Condor' service, but these trains still used two-axle wagons and it was not until the Beeching Report of 1963 that a modern alternative began to take shape, with its recommendation to build 55 strategically located terminals throughout the country that would be linked by a network of 'Liner' trains formed of bogie wagons able to carry the larger 10ft, 20ft and 30ft containers then under development.

The first Freightliner service, between Glasgow and London, began in November 1965 and by 1974 there were some 32 terminals owned either by Freightliner (24), the port companies (four), or shipping consortia (four), while the number of containers carried on rail had increased from 27,000 in 1966 to more than 630,000. In large part this increase was driven by the rapid expansion of worldwide containerisation and as the 1970s progressed the focus of Freightliner's operations would move away from its domestic business and towards the international market.

With improvements to Britain's roads customers were now finding that, once loaded, it was becoming more economical and timely for a container to complete its entire journey by road rather than take it to the nearest Freightliner terminal, whereas, by its very nature, the transshipment of a seaborne container once it arrived at a port was an inevitability. Consequently, while domestic traffic had soon levelled out, and plans to open additional regional Freightliner terminals at places such as Carlisle, Chester and Oxford were abandoned, additional services were soon required to run from the burgeoning container ports of Felixstowe, Southampton and Tilbury. While in 1968 almost half of all Freightliner trains had been running between inland terminals, by 1989 that figure had fallen to 15% and many of these services were conveying deep sea traffic which would be combined with another working before final delivery to a port.

The increasing dominance of international traffic also had an impact on the containers in use, with the 10ft boxes initially built for Freightliner slowly disappearing as the convenience of standardising on 20ft and 40ft containers was recognised. Furthermore, an important feature of the system was the stackability of the containers, whether on board ship or at a terminal, and so it was not

To provide as many connections as possible, portion working was once a common feature of many Freightliner services, and although this practice has declined in recent years, Crewe Basford Hall yard remains an important Freightliner base and interchange point. FFA 'Inner' No. 602353, loaded with two Hapag-Lloyd boxes, and recently arrived from Coatbridge, was waiting to be forwarded to Tilbury when photographed at Crewe on June 3, 2001.

long before the frameless tank containers had either been withdrawn or confined to dedicated workings within Britain. By the 1980s the fall in domestic traffic also resulted in the closure of many inland terminals and those at Aberdeen, Dudley, Dundee, Edinburgh, Hull, Longsight, Newcastle, Nottingham, Sheffield, Stockton and Swansea had all gone by the end of the decade.

However, on the plus side, Liverpool's Seaforth Dock benefited from a Section 8 Grant towards the cost of a new rail-connected terminal which opened in 1979, while a new Cleveland container terminal was opened in 1989 at Wilton on land belonging to ICI, and the last decade of the century also brought increased services to many of the remaining terminals, particularly those at Barton Dock, Coatbridge, Garston, Leeds and Trafford Park.

Opened in 1969 by Overseas Containers Ltd. (a consortia of the four shipping lines P&O, British & Commonwealth, Furness Withy and Alfred Holt, all of whom traded particularly with the Far East, Australasia and South Africa) the privately owned Containerbase at Barton Dock, situated on the western fringe of Manchester and close to Trafford Park industrial estate, was initially served by an out-and-back service to Southampton.

By 2001 Barton Dock was the originating point for four daily Freightliner workings, with two for Southampton and one each for Felixstowe and Tilbury. However, unlike in its early years, where the balance of traffic at Containerbase had comprised around 55% outgoing and 45% incoming, by the 1990s imports had begun to dominate so that by 2001 they outnumbered exports by more than three to one, a pattern that could be reflected at every container terminal reflecting the decline in the country's manufacturing base.

The opening of the Channel Tunnel in 1994 also gave a considerable boost to container traffic, with new terminals being built at Daventry, Hams Hall and Wakefield, and existing terminals expanded to handle the expected increase in business. With

The Class 47s that Freightliner inherited from Railfreight Distribution in 1996 were not in the best of health and between 1997 and 1999 12 would be refurbished at Brush Traction's Falcon Works in Loughborough. Fitted with reconditioned EMD power plants, the modified locomotives were reclassified as Class 57s and painted in Freightliner's new green and yellow livery. No. 57004 'Freightliner Quality' heads 4029, the 12.47 SO Trafford Park to Southampton MCT, through Deansgate station in September 1999.

hindsight the forecasts for freight through the tunnel, whether conveyed in containers or conventional wagons, can be seen to have been over optimistic, but while direct through services between Britain and Europe failed to meet expectations, several of the recently opened inland terminals began handling increasing amounts of domestic and deep sea traffic.

This development gathered pace from the late-1990s when English Welsh & Scottish Railway, the Wisconsin Central subsidiary who in 1997 had acquired Railfreight Distribution's Channel Tunnel business to add to its earlier acquisition of the three Trainload Freight companies, introduced new container trains to Daventry, Hams Hall, Immingham, Seaforth and Wakefield. Rail activity at Daventry would increase further in the following decade with the commencement of the Direct Rail Services-hauled Tesco container trains, while today

eight Anglo-Scottish services operate between Daventry and Scotland conveying traffic for a number of different customers. With the long-standing working from Felixstowe and Southampton continuing to flourish, new container services to London Gateway, Liverpool Seaforth and Doncaster iPort having all commenced in recent years, and with the development of another inland terminal at Castle Donnington well advanced, it can be fairly said that the container is now king.

The OCL Containerbase at Barton Dock had two long sidings, each capable of accommodating 15 bogie flat wagons, as well as a short stub track intended for a future expansion which was never implemented. The container trains were worked between Containerbase and BR's Trafford Park West Sidings by Manchester Ship Canal Co. locomotives and on May 2, 1992 the MSC's Nos. D6, DH23 and DH26 wait to leave the 'Base' with 4067, the evening service for Southampton MCT. At the time, double or triple-heading this heavy train along the MSC-owned branch line was common practice.

Looking back from the leading locomotive as a pair of the MSC's 255 bhp 4wDH Sentinels tackle the stiff climb up to Waters Meeting with 4094, the 11.45 SO from Barton Dock to Southampton MCT, on November 24, 1990.

Containers from across the world were regularly to be seen on the Barton Dock trains, but one of the less common visitors was the 20ft box belonging to the OT Africa Line, a shipping line established in 1975 following the discovery of oil in Nigeria, seen loaded on to FSA No. 608336 outside Containerbase on May 2, 2007. Sharing space on the wagon were 20ft Mitsui O.S.K. and Nippon Yusen boxes, the 20-footers often being backloaded from Barton Dock with either scrap metal or waste paper. The FSA was one of 700 new bogie conflats that BR had purchased for Freightliner traffic from the French wagon builder Arbel Fauvet in 1991.

Among the more unusual commodities handled at Barton Dock were containers of 'yellow cake', a uranium ore concentrate which once-purified is used in the production of fuel rods for nuclear power stations. On April 30, 1997 Class 90 No. 90150 heads a late-running Tilbury to Barton Dock Freightliner through Manchester Oxford Road, with the leading wagon carrying three Russian Railway 20ft containers loaded with 'yellow cake'. Upon arrival at Containerbase the containers would be forwarded by road to British Nuclear Fuels' Springfield Works outside Preston.

A total of 552 10ft Freightliner box containers would be built between 1964 and 1968, and they remained a feature on domestic services until the early 1980s. Container No. 02G73, built at Horwich Works in 1967, is pictured awaiting disposal at Trafford Park West Sidings in February 1988. For much of the previous decade it had been used as a static store at the nearby Trafford Park Freightliner terminal. *(©Trevor Mann)*

BELOW: By the 1980s 20ft and 40ft boxes dominated most Freightliner workings with deep sea traffic making up the majority of the containers being handled. In September 1984 Class 33 No. 33004 heads 4M60, the 12.34 SO Southampton Maritime Terminal to Birmingham Lawley Street, at Radley, with a mix of OCL, Ben Line and Nedlloyd Lines boxes in the consist.

(©Trevor Mann collection)

By 2012 all the Freightliner workings to Barton Dock had been withdrawn, leaving the branch with just a solitary GBRf-hauled service from Felixstowe. To work the branch GBRf acquired a pair of Class 09s, Nos. 09002 and 09009, and the latter is seen here leaving Containerbase with 4L18, the 11.28 to Felixstowe North, on February 3, 2012. From January 2013 this train operated from the Trafford Park Euro-Terminal and the Barton Dock branch was closed.

The opening of the Channel Tunnel in 1994 brought a considerable boost to intermodal traffic, with trains initially running from Birmingham (Lawley Street), Liverpool (Seaforth Dock), Manchester (Trafford Park), Mossend and Wakefield to Wembley. At Wembley the 'Euro-Twin' wagons would be remarshalled before continuing their journey, via Dollands Moor, to one of a dozen continental destinations. Class 90 No. 90133 heads 4A13, the 13.10 SO Trafford Park to Wembley, through Stafford on September 22, 1997.

The Manchester Ship Canal Company's Barton Dock branch, which ran from British Rail's Trafford Park West sidings to Containerbase, crossed the Bridgewater Canal at Waters Meeting via a bridge over which larger locomotives were not permitted. Consequently, after the MSCs own locomotives were withdrawn, a pair of hired-in Andrew Barclay 0-6-0DH locomotives and then Class 08s took over the task of hauling the container trains along the branch. Renumbered as MSC 1 and named 'Emily', works No. AB660/built 1982/rebuilt HAB6769 in 1990, crosses Park Road, part way along the branch, with the 11.30 SX departure for Southampton MCT on February 23, 2005.

Manchester's other Freightliner terminal at Longsight opened in 1966 with services to Glasgow and London. From 1974 4S57, the 18.48 Longsight to Glasgow, would be diesel-hauled only as far as Wigan where a pair of electrics then took over for the remainder of the run to Scotland. Here Class 86 No. 86032 and Class 87 No. 87023 prepare to head north from Wigan Springs Branch in May 1977, with 4S57 conveying a mix of Freightliner boxes and CPC tank containers for Glasgow. The blue striped livery seen on the first box behind the locomotives was carried by containers allocated to British Rail rather than to Freightliner, including those belonging to BR's Shipping Division, while the black and white frameless 30ft Corn Product Co. tank containers were a common sight on the Longsight to Glasgow Freightliner, conveying dextrose produced at the CPC works in Trafford Park, which was destined to pharmaceutical manufacturers and food producers in Scotland.

A Kalmar container handler unloads an Alberti & Santi swap-body at Daventry International Rail Terminal in July 2000. Swap-bodies had been uncommon on British freight workings until the opening of the Channel Tunnel.

With a solution having finally been found to their track circuit immunisation problems, Raifreight Distribution's Class 92s were finally cleared to work traffic along the West Coast Main Line in 2000, while the following years the remarshalling of intermodal trains at Wembley was reduced in favour of running services directly to Dollands Moor. Class 92 No. 92041 'Vaughan Williams' heads through Crewe with 4M14, the 02.56 Dollands Moor to Trafford Park, on July 6, 2002.

The Trafford Park to Wembley/Dollands Moor intermodals were always well loaded conveying a wide range of different boxes, swap-bodies, flatracks and tank containers. Among the most striking were those operated by the French distribution company United Rouch, such as this swap-body seen aboard a Euro-Twin heading through Deansgate on its way back to Paris on May 28, 1997.

Opened in July 1972 Southampton Maritime Container Terminal quickly established itself as one of the two major port locations for Freightliner traffic and by 1985 was the originating point for trains to Barking, Barton Dock, Birmingham, Coatbridge, Garston and Leeds. Equipped with a 35-tonne Stothert & Pitt cantilever traveling crane spanning its four loop tracks, there are also four other dead-end sidings available to store additional wagons and those awaiting repair. Traffic would continue to rise during the 1990s with additional services to Crewe and Trafford Park, while Freightliner's original fleet of bogie flats was supplemented by wagons leased from Tiphook and SNCF. In this April 2002 view a French-registered bogie Euro-Twin, no longer required for Channel Tunnel traffic, awaits loading at Southampton, while beyond, the loaded train of FSA and FTA wagons will depart later in the day as 4M58, the 19.47 SX to Trafford Park, which also included portions for the terminals at Barton Dock and Garston.

The bogie Freightliner wagons were of a skeletal design and initially marshalled in sets of five wagons, each set comprising two 'outers' and three 'inners' with bar couplings rather than conventional buffer gear being used within each set, thereby reducing the tare weight. FFA 'Inner' No. 602188 is seen at Deansgate in a Trafford Park to Southampton working in May 1997.

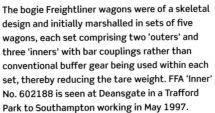

BELOW LEFT AND RIGHT: Among other uncommon loads observed in the early years of the Trafford Park to Wembley trains were these T.T.S. Tipes peak-roof containers and a TNT Express 40ft box, recorded at Deansgate and Manchester Oxford Road respectively during April 1999.

The Cawoods Container Terminal at Ellesmere Port gained a rail connection in 1986, initially to receive trainloads of export coal for Ireland, but from 1990 it also began handling Freightliner traffic and on October 18 Class 47 No. 47333 was recorded leaving with the short-lived 14.43 to Crewe Basford Hall. At Crewe the wagons would be attached to an ongoing service for Coatbridge.

A rare Habitat container shares space with a United Rouch box onboard French-registered IFA No. 33 87 4908 183-6 as it passes through Manchester Oxford Road in the consist of 4A11, the 12.32 Trafford Park to Wembley, on August 8, 1998. Well over 1,000 Euro-Twin bogie container flats were built for Channel Tunnel traffic in the 1990s and in subsequent years they have also appeared on domestic container workings and, when fitted with a low platform floor, in car traffic from Dagenham and Southampton.

Both powder and tank containers were also often to be seen being conveyed by the Trafford Park Channel Tunnel trains. Some of the powder containers were carrying abrasives (powders) destined for the Colgate toothpaste factory in Salford, while others were loaded with soda ash (sodium carbonate) for export, these having been roaded to Trafford Park Euro Terminal from one of the ICI chemical plants in Northwich. Two abrasives containers, loaded on to a Euro-Twin, head through Manchester Oxford Road on their way back to France in August 1998.

LEFT: For many years the north west of England has been home to companies involved in the production of specialist oils, and in February 2000 this 31,000-litre 'Super Heavy' Trans America 20ft tank container was recorded in the consist of the Trafford Park to Wembley service when returning to the continent after making a delivery of lubricating oil additive to a firm at Ellesmere Port.

With the River Orwell beyond, AAE Megafret No. 33 68 4909 752-0 waits to leave Ipswich Griffen Wharf on July 6, 2000. On this occasion all of the containers on the Ipswich to Ditton working were 20ft boxes loaded with imported wines and spirits. The AAE Megafret was one of the first low-deck container flats to see widespread use in Britain and by 2018 it was in service with DB, Freightliner and GBRf.

Fitted with SCT bogies the 'Shortliner' wagons are coded FWA and No. 83 70 4520 041-2 was loaded with two of the distinctive ONE boxes when recorded at Crewe in May 2019. Ocean Network Express, a joint venture combining the business of NYK, Mitsui OSK and K Line, had signed a contract with Freightliner in 2018 which was expected to see its traffic increase by more than 12% than when the three lines were operating independently.

Initially GBRf had leased a set of FCA flats from EWS, but in 2003 they began purchasing their own 60ft bogie container wagons, not only to take over the Hams Hall service, but also for use on new workings from Felixstowe to Daventry and Selby. Coded FEA No. 650013, one of their first batch of 54, built by Greenbrier, was photographed at Rugby in May 2005. Gauge enhancements on several routes meant that 9ft 6in Hi-Cube containers could now be carried on standard height conflats.

An early EWS container service was an Ipswich to Ditton train, but although loadings appeared healthy it proved to be short-lived. Class 37 No. 37669 shunts the outgoing service at Ipswich Griffen Wharf on July 6, 2000, its train comprising one Euro-Twin, two FKA low-deck twin sets and three AAE Megafrets which are out of view.

RIGHT: The FAAs were a well wagon able to accommodate either two 20ft or a single 40ft container. However, they were never popular and many spent several years in store before withdrawals commenced in 2019. FAA No. 609027 is seen at Warrington Arpley yard in June 2001.

BELOW: Following its purchase of the three trainload freight companies EWS also decided to expand into the domestic intermodal market ordering a fleet of 100 FAA and 150 FKA container flats from the Thrall works in York. Among the new container trains EWS introduced in 1999 was a Felixstowe to Wakefield working, although in competition with the long-established Freightliner service between Felixstowe and Leeds loadings were often rather sparse. Class 66 No. 66038 heads 6E45, the 02.42 Felixstowe to Wakefield Europort, through Doncaster in July 2006 with three empty FAAs at the head of the consist.

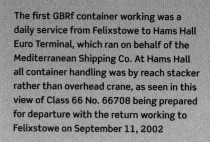

The first GBRf container working was a daily service from Felixstowe to Hams Hall Euro Terminal, which ran on behalf of the Mediterranean Shipping Co. At Hams Hall all container handling was by reach stacker rather than overhead crane, as seen in this view of Class 66 No. 66708 being prepared for departure with the return working to Felixstowe on September 11, 2002

Despite competition from other operators, Freightliner has retained the lion's share of container traffic and in 2009 purchased a fleet of 20 Class 70 locomotives from General Electric with No. 70006 seen at Crewe with 4M61, the 13.00 Southampton MCT to Trafford Park, on May 21, 2019. The train is composed almost entirely of VTG-owned Ecofret or 'Shortliner' 40ft long platform wagons, a type introduced in 2012 which maximises the platform length available within a given train, for example enabling 37 40ft boxes to be carried in comparison to a similar length train of Megafrets which can only accommodate 26.

In addition to twin-sets FEAs both Freightliner and GBRf also ordered a number of single FEAs so as to provide added flexibility in train length. All these single FEAs were to a more skeletal design than earlier container flats, as is evident in this view of No. 641024 recorded at Crewe when loaded with a 40ft Evergreen box in April 2018.

As with all freight services, the lading of each of the various Channel Tunnel intermodal trains varied according to the industrial activity to be found within the hinterland of each terminal. A regular export traffic from Parsec's Hams Hall terminal, near Coleshill, was steel pipes produced at the British Steel Bromford Bridge works as seen in this view of British-registered Euro-Twin No. 31 70 4938 011-4 recorded in August 1998.

Another steel traffic to negotiate the Channel Tunnel was the movement of 'green' steel tubes that required finishing. These were railed from northern France and Italy to Mossend and, after being tempered and threaded at Imperial Works in Airdrie, some would then be sent back to customers on the continent. IFA No. 33 87 4909 002-7 was recorded at Carlisle in the consist of a Mossend to Dollands Moor service loaded with export tubes on May 1, 1998.

Traffic on the Daventry to Coatbridge/Mossend route has taken off since Tesco first introduced its Direct Rail Services-hauled container service in 2006 and today DB and Freightliner also operate at least a daily container train on the route. All are invariably well loaded, conveying traffic on behalf of Tesco, Asda, the Malcolm Group and a host of other customers, with electric power the norm. Class 88 No. 88004 'Pandora' passes Crewe Basford Hall Junction with 4Z48, the 07.32 additional Mossend to Daventry comprised of small-wheeled bogie IDA wagons, on June 15, 2018, while on April 17, 2019 Class 90s, Nos. 90028 'Sir William McAlpine' and 90018 'The Pride of Belshill', head south from Crewe with the 06.06 Mossend to Daventry.

CHAPTER 7

The introduction of the Landfill Tax saw a drive towards more incineration of waste and in 2017, in a similar vein to Greater Manchester, the Merseyside Recycling & Waste Authority introduced its own 'Binliner' workings, running from a loading point at the old Potter Group depot in Knowsley to a recently built EfW power station at Wilton on Teesside. The Merseyside 'Binliners' were booked to run twice daily and Class 60 No. 60092 is seen powering through Patricroft with 6E26, the 10.37 Knowsley to Wilton formed of 22 FCA flats conveying 66 containers, on July 24, 2019.

Company Container Trains

Domestic refuse was a commodity to lend itself to block container operation. Not only did the use of dedicated containers, rather than conventional wagons, reduce the material's environmental impact while in transit, it also provided additional flexibility in utilising rubbish tips that might be some distance from the nearest rail siding. By the late-1970s local authorities in London and Manchester were faced with the task of handling more than half-a-million tonnes each year and so both turned to rail in order to move it to out-of-town disposal sites. The Greater Manchester Council's first 'Binliner' trains began running from Dean Lane RTP (refuse treatment plant), near Newton Heath, to the Wimpey Waste Management siding at Appley Bridge, to the west of Wigan, in 1981, the refuse being used to fill in disused mine and quarry workings. Class 31 No. 31154 passes Manchester Victoria East signalbox with 6F77, the 12.45 MWFO from Dean Lane, in October 1982, having just descended the one-in-59 incline from Miles Platting.

Following the opening of the Channel Tunnel in 1994, Ford introduced a daily train to move car parts between its plants at Dagenham and Silla, near Valencia in Spain, the predominant traffic comprising engines manufactured in Dagenham and gear boxes and transmissions produced in Bridgend. As the route involved a change of gauge at the French/Spanish border, and the sidings at Dagenham could not accept wagons of more than 9m wheelbase, some 300 new two-axle flats with moveable axles were built by Transfesa. They also supplied the purpose-built curtain-sided containers, and Class 47s Nos. 47219 and 47201 were recorded arriving at Dagenham with the train in October 1996. In recent years some non-Ford traffic (such as fruit and vegetables for UK supermarkets) has been conveyed on the Valencia to Dagenham service as far as Ripple Lane in 'Mega-Combi' 3m containers or CAI High-Cube 45ft containers.

In their early years haulage for the GMC 'Binliners' included Classes 25, 31, 37, 40 and 45, but by 1990 Class 47s and 60s were in charge. Class 47 No. 47378 leaves Appley Bridge with 6J75, the 09.00 empty containers for Dean Lane, on July 5, 1991, a couple of years before trains to Appley Bridge would cease and be replaced by workings to a new waste terminal at Roxby Gullet, near Scunthorpe.

KFA No. GMC92533, pictured passing through Stockport in the consist of a Roxby to Northenden working in July 2000, was one of 52 bogie conflats purchased by Greater Manchester Council for its 'Binliner' trains. In 2015 these would begin running to a new 121megawatt EfW (Energy from Waste) Combined Heat and Power plant at Runcorn.

Since 2016 semi-finished aluminium and finished body pressings for Jaguar Landrover have also been carried in curtain-sided containers with a daily service running from Neuss, near Düsseldorf in Germany, to Daventry and Ditton, from where the containers complete their journey by road. Standard bogie Euro-Twin and Megafret wagons are used on this service, such as FIA No. 33 70 4938 107-8 seen at Crewe in June 2018.

In the early 1990s growing concern over the environmental impact of acid rain saw the installation of flue-gas desulphurisation plants at several coal-fired power stations, where the flue gases are brought into contact with an aqueous suspension of powdered limestone. The damaging sulphur dioxide reacts with the calcium in the limestone to form desulphogypsum, a material that can be used as a supplement to natural gypsum but one which is difficult to unload from hopper or tippler wagons. Consequently when a new rail working from Drax Power Station to the British Gypsum plasterboard works at New Biggin, near Appleby, was introduced in 1994, purpose-built end-tipping 20ft containers were used. On April 11, 2007 Class 60 No. 60045 passes Ribblehead with 6E13, the 12.40 New Biggin to Milford West Sidings formed of bogie KFA wagons that were purchased new by British Gypsum in 1994.

The advantages of containerised transport were less with regard to bulk movements, but in the late-1960s container trains loaded with automotive components ran on behalf of both Chrysler and Ford. Formed of four or five sets of bogie Freightliner flats, the Chrysler trains ran between the company's works at Linwood, in Renfrewshire, and Gosford Green freight depot in Coventry, carrying body panels and gearboxes south, while transmissions, made at Chrysler's Stoke Green works in Coventry, went north. The Ford trains also carried inter-works traffic running from Halewood to the Parkeston Quay Freightliner terminal at Harwich, from where the containers were exported to Ford factories at Cologne and Saarlouis in Germany, and Genk in Belgium. Changes within the car industry saw the Chrysler trains withdrawn in 1976, but the Ford trains lasted until the early 1980s. Class 86 No. 86001 passes through Stafford with a Ford container train for Halewood in November 1983.

The switch to burning biomass at Drax and the run down of other coal-fired power stations saw the volume of desulphogypsum traffic decline, while by 2018 the remaining workings were shared between DB and GBRf. British Gypsum's own KFA wagons had also given way to Megafrets, as seen in this view of Class 66 No. 66708 'Jayne' at Hellifield with a working from New Biggin on April 8, 2019.

RIGHT: Tioxide's Pyewipe works at Grimsby processed imported ilmenite ore to produce titanium dioxide, a pigment widely used in the manufacture of paint, plastics, synthetic fibres, ceramics and cosmetics. The process generated several by-products, including red gypsum, an inert material suitable for landfill, and once a new gypsum separation plant was opened on-site in 1993 this was railed to the new waste disposal facility at Roxby. The train usually ran three days a week and Class 60 No. 60051 'Mary Somerville' is seen arriving back at Grimsby with 6D86, the 11.20 empty containers from Roxby, on October 31, 1995.

RIGHT: The red gypsum was carried in new 20ft open-top containers lettered for Tioxide, with a pool of 16 Railease bogie flats hired for the traffic. KFA No. RLS92555 is pictured at Grimsby in July 1997.

Innovative Intermodal

In an effort to capture a larger share of the domestic consumer goods market, several innovative intermodal wagons were tested in the early 1990s, although disappointingly none met with any long-term success. Most numerous were the 100 bogie Tiphook Piggyback 'Swing-Decks' first leased by Charterail in 1991 to carry specially designed road trailers loaded with pet food from the Pedigree Petfood works at Melton Mowbray to Cricklewood. The wagons were 53ft 4in long with a carrying capacity of 37 tonnes and had a hinged deck that could be swung to the side so that a purpose-built road trailer could be reversed onboard. Piggyback KOA No. 83 70 4798 014-4 is pictured being loaded at Melton Mowbray in September 1991.

Charterail also introduced an Anglo-Scottish service running between Glasgow and Cricklewood, which was formed of Tiphook Piggyback 'Swing-Decks', conveying various commodities including bagged sugar, soft drinks and paper. Unfortunately loadings on the Anglo-Scottish service proved disappointing and Charterail soon ran into financial difficulties with the wagons going into store. KOA No. 83 70 4798 017-7 was spotted at Warrington Arpley when en route to Glasgow in September 1992.

Another attempt to carry road trailers were the two 'Eurospine' wagons built by Babcock Rail at its Rosyth workshop in 1996. Each comprised four 'Piggyback' platforms, identified as A, B, C and D, but with a single TOPS number for the entire set, designed to accommodate top-lift UK-gauge low-height trailers up to 44ft 6in long or 40/45ft ISO containers. Each platform could carry 36 tonnes and after extensive testing with Russell curtain-sided trailers, the two 'Eurospine' sets were put to work on a new overnight service between Willesden and Mossend carrying purpose-built Parcelforce trailers. In 1999 a further 20 Eurospine sets were built at Thrall's Tatravagonka Works in the Czech Republic, but rather than increase as anticipated, the Parcelforce contract came to an unexpected end in 2002. The 'Eurospines' were then briefly used in container traffic from Southampton before their eventual withdrawal in 2016. A new FHA No. PIGY97001 is pictured at Warrington Dallam freight depot when undergoing tests in October 1996.

At the same time as Charterail was leasing the Tiphook Piggyback wagons it was also developing its version of the Road-Railer. This was originally a North American concept, first developed by the Chesapeake & Ohio Railway in 1956, and with which British Rail had dabbled in the early 1960s. However, the small 11-tonne BR vehicles had never entered commercial service and the concept was apparently forgotten, until in 1991 Charterail introduced a set of three 20-tonne trailers running on four specially designed bogies and adaptors. Having been sidelined with the collapse of Charterail in 1992, in 1996 Transrail began using the Road-Railer between Aberdeen and Northampton carrying paper from the Arjo Wiggins mill at Dyce and the Federal Tait mill at Port Elphinstone. They also ran from the Tibbett & Britten depot at Daventry to Mossend loaded with domestic appliances, but unfortunately the cost of specialist equipment, the time-consuming transfer from road to rail, and the extra weight of the trailers' road gear being carried when in rail mode, all limited interest and by May 1999 the vehicles were out of use. Both solid and curtain-sided Road-Railer trailers were used as seen in these views of the bogies and trailers recorded at Melton Mowbray in July 1991 and at Northampton in October 1996.

CHAPTER 8

Reefers on Rail

RIGHT: Loads that required refrigeration or temperature-controlled conditions were carried in either specialist containers or in Interfrigo vans, registered by the Belgian, Hungarian and Italian railways, and until the early-1990s Interfrigo vans would be a common sight in Britain arriving via the Dunkirk to Dover train ferry. Class 09 No. 09008 shunts Belgian Interfrigo vans and a Transfesa van into the transit shed alongside the old linkspan sidings at Dover in June 1976. (©Geoff Corner collection)

Supermarket traffic on rail has grown considerably since the turn of the Millennium and while most is carried in dry boxes and swap-bodies it is usual to find one or two Stobart/ Tesco reefers, fitted with Thermo King SLXe diesel-electric refrigeration units, on many of the workings between Daventry and Mossend. Like the Unit45 containers the Stobart/Tesco reefers are 45ft long and fitted with Thermo King refrigeration units, but they are turned out in a rather more elaborate and attractive livery. Container No. ESCU480644-0, loaded on to IKA Megafret No. 33 68 4909 439-4, heads through Patricroft on August 2, 2019 in the consist of a diverted Mossend to Daventry service. Although reefers still occasionally turn up on other workings, they are now predominantly to be seen on long-distance domestic intermodal services such as those running between Daventry and Scotland, as well as on workings to and from the major container ports of Felixstowe and Southampton.

Today's refrigerated containers are all fitted with a diesel-powered compressor, either bolted to the end or integrated within the frame, and can maintain a -35°C set point for deep frozen cargoes. Some also have an air management system which monitors and adjusts the internal levels of CO2 and O2, thus maintaining these gases at the optimal levels when loaded with fresh produce such as fruit, vegetables and flowers. Loaded on to FEA No. 630033 a Unit45 45ft high-cube reefer, capable of accommodating 33 euro-pallets, is seen departing from Containerbase in the consist of 4L34, the short-lived 10.24 Barton Dock to Ripple Lane working, on May 4, 2011. These modern reefers are designed for very long-haul operations being fitted with a 250-litre diesel tank.

By the mid-1990s the Interfrigo vans had all but disappeared from Britain's rail network with most refrigerated traffic having been containerised and the ABC Container Line of Antwerp was one of several companies to operate a fleet of 20ft frozen food containers. These were fitted with a diesel-powered compressor unit which, operating intermittently much like a domestic fridge, cut in and out to maintain the required internal temperature. Two ABC reefers, loaded on to FSA No. 608272, pass Allerton East Junction in the consist of a local Garston to Seaforth Dock Freightliner trip working on April 12, 1995. From Seaforth the ABC containers would be shipped to Dublin.

By the late-1980s it was only the larger 12.7m-long Italian Interfrigo vans that still visited Britain, loaded with either soft fruits or frozen meats, while they might also carry the occasional backload such as milk products from Stranraer or potatoes from Aberdeen. In August 1988 IIB No. 03 83 8089 771-0 is pictured at Warrington Dallam awaiting internal cleaning before being despatched to Aberdeen Guild Street FD for loading with seed potatoes destined for France.

One of the more unusual loads to be imported in Interfrigo vans was frozen pigs lungs, which until 1990 were railed from Kolding in Denmark to the Pedigree Petfood factory at Melton Mowbray. The vans, which could each carry approximately 800 frozen lungs, were unloaded at the small goods yard adjacent to Melton Mowbray station, and on March 17, 1988 Class 47 No. 47311 had just delivered two Interfrigos while working the Speedlink trip from Toton.

CHAPTER 9

Locomotives intended for departmental service were repainted in a new Civil Engineers yellow and grey 'Dutch' scheme although, like those in the various sub-sector liveries, it was not uncommon to find them hauling other freight trains. This photograph, taken from the famous Platform 11 at Manchester Victoria on April 26, 1991, sees Class 31 No. 31306 waiting its next turn of duty in Road 19, also known as the "Wall Side" road, while beyond the appropriately named Class 47 No. 47333 *'Civil Link'* is stabled beneath the out-of-use luggage bridge.

Locomotives and Liveries

With the Modernisation Plan of 1955 having committed BR to replacing steam as quickly as possible, it soon placed numerous orders for a range of diesel locomotive designs, both for shunting and yard duties as well as for main line traffics. Indeed, even before 1955 diesel shunters were being built in considerable numbers and eventually BR was to purchase shunters from nine different builders to work at small and large goods depots and docks throughout the country. However, only a few years after many had been delivered, the implementation of the Beeching Report, with its recommendation to rationalise freight yards and reduce local trip workings, would make lots of them redundant, with most of the smaller numeric classes either withdrawn or else sold on to industrial users. For its lighter shunting duties, and at locations where tight curves required short wheelbase locomotives, British Rail decided to standardise on the Gardner-engined 204 bhp 0-6-0DM Class 03, while the English Electric 350 bhp 0-6-0DE, which would become the Class 08s and 09s, became its general-purpose diesel shunter.

It would be a similar story regarding the main line locomotive fleet where some of the earlier designs had proved to be unreliable or under-powered, while by the 1970s the diesel hydraulics originally favoured by the Western Region had been deemed as non-standard and

were also heading, somewhat prematurely, for the scrapyard. However, despite such cutbacks, the BR fleet in the early-1970s was still one of considerable diversity and the Ian Allan Combined Volume for 1972 listed some 18 main line and eight shunting classes still in service.

Furthermore, the majority of the main line types had been designed as mixed traffic locomotives that could be routinely allocated to either passenger, parcels, or freight, although by the 1970s a handful, such as the Class 20s and the sub-Class 47/3s, which had been fitted with slow-speed control for hauling MGR coal trains, were now concentrated on freight work.

However, it would not be until the introduction of the Class 56 in 1976 and the Class 58 in 1982 that BR began purchasing locomotives specifically intended for its freight business and these would be followed in 1989 by the Class 60s whose arrival almost coincided with the sectorisation of freight operations, that added a further level of resource dedication to the locomotive fleet. In 1994 the run-up to privatisation saw the establishment of three shadow freight franchises, Loadhaul, Mainline and Transrail, with each receiving a share of both the BR locomotive and wagon fleets, but these separate organisations would soon disappear

with their purchase by the Wisconsin Central Railroad subsidiary English Welsh and Scottish Railways in 1997.

The new owners lost no time in replacing much of the ageing locomotive fleet with an order for 250 new Class 66s to be built by General Motors at its plant in London, Ontario, Canada. Derived from GM's earlier Class 59 design, which was already in operation with ARC, Foster Yeoman and National Power, the 3,300bhp Class 66s entered service with EWS between 1998 and 2000 and the type would prove popular with other railfreight operators Freightliner, GBRf, DRS and Jarvis Rail, all subsequently placing orders for their own Class 66s.

Today more than 85% of all freight traffic is Class 66-hauled, although a handful of Class 56s and 60s can still be found at work for Colas and GBRf and both Freightliner and Colas also operate a small number of the General Electric-built Class 70s. Both Freightliner and Deutsche Bahn, who purchased EWS in 2007, also still utilise their allocation of Class 90s on WCML freight work, but it is Direct Rail Services, who first entered the train operating business in 1995, that operates the most varied fleet ranging from a number of Class 20s and 37s built in the 1950s and early 1960s to the latest dual-powered Class 88s built at Stadler Rail's Valencia works in 2015/16.

From the numerous small shunting locomotives introduced in the 1950s BR would settle upon its own 204 bhp 0-6-0DM Class 03 as the favoured type for light shunting duties, with the works at Doncaster and Swindon turning out some 230 of them between 1955 and 1960. Allocated to all but the Scottish Region the Class 03s were a common sight in the 1960s shunting in local goods yards or acting as station pilots, but they were withdrawn steadily from 1968 and by 1983 only 29, mostly dual-braked, examples remained in service with BR. These included three that were allocated to Birkenhead Mollington St TMD in October 1981 in order to take over the remaining freight-shunting duties around the nearby docks following the cessation of Rea Bulk Handling's rail operations. Class 03 No. 03170 is pictured at Birkenhead Cavendish Sidings in April 1986 but by March 1989, following a downturn in grain traffic to the mills at Birkenhead, it was moved to Chester TMD for storage and later that year was sold to Otis Euro Transrail to work at their Ordsall Lane rail terminal in Salford.

Also powered by a Gardner 8L3 204 bhp engine and weighing just 29 tonnes 15cwt the similar Drewry Class 04 0-6-0 diesel mechanical shunters, built between 1952 and 1961, fared rather less well and all 140 had been withdrawn by the end of 1972. However, it was a lack of work that had led to their demise on BR and 62 Class 04s would be sold for industrial service, their purchasers including the Ford Motor Co., the NCB, the Llanelli Steel Co. and the British Sugar Corporation. In 1969 the former No. D2324, works No. DC2705/RSH8183, built 1961, was sold to G.W. Talbot Ltd. for further use at Aylesbury Coal Concentration Depot, where it worked until 1990 before being moved to Redland Aggregates at Mountsorrel. Repainted in Redland's green livery it was photographed at Mountsorrel in January 1994.

BELOW: The arrival of the Class 58s in 1982 coincided with the establishment of 'Railfreight' as the freight division of British Rail complete with its own new 'Railfreight Grey' livery, the first break from the almost universal application of Rail Blue which had been introduced back in 1965. More usually found hauling MGR coal trains in the East Midlands, the miners' strike of 1984/85 saw the Class 58s spread their wings and on April 24, 1985 No. 58011 was spotted heading through Guide Bridge with 7M60, the 12.46 Ashburys to Toton Speedlink, which on this occasion was formed of a single ZDA 'Bass' (ox-OCA) loaded with brake blocks for Derby Loco Works.

The 350 bhp 0-6-0 diesel electric shunter, of which almost 1000 would be built between 1952 and 1962, became the standard BR design, although their numbers would also decline steadily from the early-1970s as freight yards closed and wagonload operations gradually disappeared. However, locations such as wagon repair depots still required the services of a shunting locomotive and on July 24, 1990 Class 08 No. 08622 was busy shunting at Motherwell WRD.

Gradually 'Railfreight Grey' livery was applied to other locomotives allocated to freight traffic, such as Class 47 No. 47280 *'Pedigree'* which is seen at Chester on July 1, 1986 at the head of 6E36, the 07.00 empty Petroleum Coke train which ran twice weekly from the Anglesey Aluminium smelter at Holyhead to Humber Oil Refinery at Immingham. The locomotive had been named earlier that year at Melton Mowbray, home to Pedigree Petfoods.

However, many locomotives remained in Rail Blue livery including the 12 Class 25/3s which, at the end of 1985, had been re-classified as 25/9s with the intention that they would be used to haul traffic on behalf of the Industrial Minerals Division. Their intended workings were the seasonal movement of rock salt from Over & Wharton to Scotland but in practice they could be found handling a variety of local freights around the north west, such as the daily Dee Marsh to Warrington Speedlink trip, seen here waiting time at Chester behind Class 25s Nos. 25905 and 25906 on July 1, 1986.

The next significant development came in 1987 when Railfreight was divided into sectors, this being accompanied by the introduction of a new triple-grey livery which was commonly applied to all the traffic sectors' locomotives but embellished with specific sector logos as appropriate. Developed by the Roundel Design Group, these logos were all similar in outline, featuring bold colours and geometric shapes that related to the various traffics carried. For example, the emblem for Railfreight Construction sported blue and yellow blocks, while that for Railfreight Metals had sharp blue and yellow chevrons and the Railfreight Coal logo featured four stylised lumps of coal in black on a yellow background. Railfreight Distribution's locomotives, which handled wagonload traffic and container trains, sported red diamonds on a yellow background, as illustrated by Class 37 No. 37059 *'Port of Tilbury'* photographed at Motherwell TMD in July 1991, while those allocated to Railfreight Petroleum had a wavy liquid design in blue and yellow as seen on Class 47 No. 47380 at Eccles on March 22, 1991.

Epitomising the mixed traffic nature of the BR locomotive fleet is this view of Class 50 No. 50018 *'Resolution'* in BR large logo blue livery seen passing Horse Cove, near Dawlish, with a rake of empty Seacow ballast hoppers on August 21, 1985. Built in 1967/68, primarily to haul passenger trains on the West Coast Main Line north of Crewe, the Class 50s were no strangers to freight traffic, having already seen use on such workings while they were on the London Midland Region before their transfer to the Western Region in the mid-1970s.

LEFT: Also formed during the run-up to privatisation in order to take over the movement of nuclear material from British Rail was Direct Rail Services, then a subsidiary of BNFL. Initially DRS purchased 15 Class 20s from RFS Engineering that had previously been used on Channel Tunnel work, and after being refurbished and fitted with modified cab equipment by Brush Traction at Loughborough they were first put to work on the local low-level waste trip between Sellafield and Drigg. Class 20/3 No. 20303, in original DRS livery, is seen at Sellafield in May 2005.

In 1994 yet more new liveries would appear when, in the run-up to privatisation, BR's trainload freight operations were split into the three shadow freight franchises. Transrail, whose operating area encompassed Scotland, Wales and the western side of England, would make do with embellishing the existing triple-grey livery with their large T logo, whereas Loadhaul, who were based in the north east of England, and Mainline, whose main operating area stretched from South Yorkshire to Kent, both chose to completely repaint many of their allocated locomotives. In 'aircraft blue', with silver bodyside stripe and 'rolling wheels' logo, Mainline's Class 37 No. 37198 leaves Longport in June 1996 with a train of discharged Carless petroleum distillate tanks destined for Harwich, while Class 56 No. 56112 was still sporting the Loadhaul black and orange scheme when pictured arriving at Tees Dock with a train of bogie potash covhops from Boulby in August 2001.

One of the most significant impacts of railfreight privatisation was the subsequent introduction of the General Motors-built Class 66 locomotives. After EWS placed an order for 250 in 1998 all of the other major freight operating companies would follow their example, so that by spring 2016 a total of 485 had been put to work in Britain. Among them were Freightliner's 25 Class 66/6s delivered between 2000 and 2007 which had a lower gear ratio and therefore higher tractive effort than other Class 66s, albeit with a reduced maximum speed of only 65mph. Class 66/6 No. 66607 approaches Hyde Junction to join the old Woodhead route while running light engine from Tunstead Quarry to the Freightliner operating base at Guide Bridge in August 2019.

Railfreight privatisation in 1996 brought with it not only many new locomotives, but a plethora of different paint schemes. Not only did each of the new operating companies quickly adopt their own individual colours, but they also indulged in painting some locomotives in one-off liveries, most usually in recognition of the acquisition of new business. One of the first of these was GB Railfreight's Class 66 No. 66709, which in 2002 appeared in 'Medite' colours to mark the company's first Intermodal contract which saw new container services introduced from Felixstowe to Hams Hall and Selby on behalf of the Mediterranean Shipping Company. That same year GBRf also began operating its first bulk freight contract with a West Burton PS to Newbiggin working for British Gypsum, seen here behind No. 66709 at Doncaster on July 12, 2006.

BELOW: Both Freightliner and DB Schenker also chose to paint a handful of their locomotives in customer-dedicated liveries. DB's Class 66 No. 66005 had recently been repainted in 'Maritime' livery and named *'Maritime Intermodal One'* when spotted leaving Milford West Sidings with a train of empty biomass hoppers for Immingham Docks in June 2019.

By the mid-1960s the very attractive 'Electric Blue' livery that had first adorned the early West Coast Main Line electric locomotives had been replaced by the rather more prosaic 'Rail Blue', although at least the distinctive white cab roof and window surrounds would remain for a few more years. AL5 No. E3084, one of 40 25kV electrics built at Doncaster Works between 1961 and 1964, heads south through Watford with 4E09, the 12.07 Halewood to Dagenham, conveying automotive components for the Ford Motor Co. on January 11, 1966. Under the TOPS renumbering scheme this locomotive became Class 85 No. 85029 in October 1974 and was eventually withdrawn in May 1988.

In 2017 Direct Rail Services introduced the Class 88, an electro-diesel development of its earlier diesel-powered Class 68. Built by Stadler Rail in Spain, the 10 Class 88s produce 5,400 bhp when operating under AC electrical power, while they are also equipped with a Caterpillar C27 12-cylinder 940 bhp diesel engine that is powerful enough to haul a train on its own. Consequently the Class 88s can work heavy freights into and out of unelectrified terminals before switching to electric mode once they reach the main line, while at the same time they are powerful enough to handle the short nuclear flask trains also operated by DRS, which are always hauled by a pair of locomotives. Seven of the 10 Class 88s are named after figures from Greek or Roman mythology, repeating names previously carried by Class 76 and 77 Woodhead electric locomotives, and Class 88 No. 88009 'Diana' (named after the Roman goddess of the hunt) is pictured heading the diverted 4M27, 05.48 Mossend to Daventry intermodal service, through Patricroft station on July 25, 2019.

It would be some years after the completion of the WCML electrification in 1974 before other trunk routes went under the wires and consequently the only new batch of electric locomotives built between 1975 and 1993 were the 50 Class 90s. This 5,000 bhp design, introduced in 1987, was intended for both express passenger and heavy freight work, but following the sectorisation of BR 26 were dedicated to freight traffic. They were reclassified as Class 90/1 after undergoing a number of modifications that included reducing their maximum speed to 75mph and isolating the electric train supply as well as being renumbered 90125-150. Initially repainted in Railfreight Distribution two-tone grey livery, Nos. 90128, 90129 and 90130 would later each receive a different continentally inspired livery and Class 90 No. 90129 'Frachtverbindungen' had been painted in Deutsche Bahn red when recorded at Deansgate with the 12.10 Trafford Park to Dollands Moor Channel Tunnel service on May 28, 1997. Some 12 years later, following the takeover of EWS by DB and subsequent change of name to DB Schenker, this red livery would also begin to appear on the company's Class 59s, 60s and 66s.

Considerably less numerous than the Class 66, and evidently less successful, was the 3690 bhp Class 70 manufactured by General Electric at its works in Erie, Pennsylvania. Similar in appearance to a Class 58, with a hood unit and narrow body typical of locomotive types in use in North America, in all some 20 Class 70s were introduced by Freightliner in 2009, followed by 17 for Colas that were delivered between 2014 and 2017. Colas Class 70 No. 70813 waits time in Hellifield Up Goods Loops with 6J37, the 12.58 Carlisle Yard to Chirk timber train, on August 10, 2018.

CHAPTER 10

Wagon Repairs

Following railfreight privatisation those repair facilities to remain in use were often upgraded, usually with a larger hoist, some form of cover and more storage capability. At Warrington Arpley the small wagon repair siding previously used, situated to the west of the WCML, was replaced by a covered facility built close to the new locomotive fuelling point on the western edge of the yard, and in October 2004 a bogie Tiphook (ex-VTG) ferry van can be seen under the overall roof near to the wagon hoist with the loco fuelling point beyond.

In 1974 British Rail still had more than 80 locations across the country where wagon repairs and maintenance were undertaken. These included large wagon repair depots, such as those situated at Cardiff Cathays, Carlisle Currock, Chester, Dunfermline Townhill, Exmouth Junction, Motherwell, New Cross Gate, Peterborough, Sheffield Darnall, Swansea, Thornaby, Toton and York, all of which were fully equipped to undertake all levels of repairs including major rebuilds, to smaller facilities like those at Tonbridge, Skipton and Warrington which might often comprise no more than a couple of uncovered sidings where basic running repairs, such as wheelset and brake replacements, could be completed. However, as freight traffic declined a number of WRDs were closed during the 1980s, while following sectorisation those to remain open became more specialised in the vehicles they maintained. For example, the works at Carlisle Currock took over responsibility for almost all Railfreight Distribution's fleet of opens and vans, while Thornaby WRD concentrated on the metal sector's wagon fleet.

LEFT: Chester Wagon Repair Depot carried out work on a wide range of wagons and on June 30, 1979 a BR Presflo from the pool based at Tunnel Cement's Padeswood Works at Penyffordd, together with a 16-ton Mineral, an unfitted Brake Van and Vanfit No. B785585 were all awaiting attention.

By the 1990s the workload at Chester WRD almost exclusively involved departmental vehicles, as is evident in this April 1995 view when it was Salmon, Sealion, Sole and Turbots awaiting repair.

RIGHT: To save space many WRDs were equipped with a wagon traverser to move wagons from one road to another. Rudd No. DB972090 takes a ride on the 1958-built machine provided at Chester in June 1993. Unfortunately Chester WRD was one of many to be closed following railfreight privatisation.

In addition to the WRDs there were also several locations around the rail network, often close to major freight yards, where minor wagon repairs could be undertaken. At Tonbridge West Yard three sidings were set aside for wagon repairs and while they predominantly handled departmental stock, occasionally BR revenue and privately owned wagons would also receive attention. In June 1986 No. APCM19564, one of the PGA gypsum hoppers allocated to the Mountfield to Northfleet traffic, awaits a new wheelset at Tonbridge, while the 6½-tonne Cowans Sheldon manual crane, internal user No.083332, ex-ADS1854, was based there for many years to assist in such operations.

At Warrington Arpley a couple of short sidings on the opposite side of the WCML to the main yard were used for wagon repairs, although facilities were basic with just an area of hard standing, a lifting frame and an old container to provide for the storage of brake hoses and basic tools. At such locations any wagon passing through the area that was found to be in need of running repairs could turn up and on a rather wet August 7, 1980 it was the turn of the Associated Octel Co's 20-ton ethylene dibromide tank No. AO47079, while on April 18, 1987 Railease's china clay PRA No. RLS6305 was spotted with a damaged brake lever on the ground.

When BR had introduced its Merry-Go-Round coal hoppers in the 1960s it also opened a handful of new wagon repair depots dedicated to maintaining these wagons. One such facility was located at Knottingley and when the HAA two-axle MGR hoppers were replaced by new EWS-owned bogie HTA coal hoppers they also visited Knottingley for maintenance, as seen in this August 2001 view of the two-road WRD.

A handful of smaller private wagon repair companies could also be found in the 1980s including the South Staffs Wagon Co. which had works at Norton Junction, near Cannock, and at Tipton, and C.C. Crump at Connah's Quay. Given its geographical location along the north Wales coastline and between the Associated Octel works at Amlwch and Ellesmere Port, Crump handled much of the routine maintenance on the Octel wagon fleet and liquid chlorine tank No. AO55344 was recorded in the works yard at Connah's Quay on June 3, 1988. Note the grounded BR ferry van body which was used as a store for bags of shot-blasting grit. Unfortunately work here plummeted in the early 1990s after the withdrawal of much of the Associated Octel fleet and the site closed soon afterwards.

By the 1990s some of the larger railfreight customers had begun to undertake most of their wagon maintenance themselves and at ARC's Whatley Quarry a small repair shop was provided just outside the main quarry loading area. A pair of the company's 102-tonne glw bogie hoppers, one of the first types to be fitted with low track force bogies, stands alongside the spare wheelsets at Whatley in July 1996.

LEFT: Until the late-1990s most maintenance of privately owned wagons was undertaken either by the wagon owners themselves or by their lessors. In the 1960s Wagon Repairs Ltd, originally established in 1918 to provide maintenance and repair for several wagon manufacturers including the Gloucester RC&W Co. and Hurst Nelson, had become part of the Charles Roberts group and in subsequent years further amalgamations and takeovers would see it pass through the hands of Procor and Marcroft Engineering. In the 1980s its largest works at Stoke-on-Trent, then operating under the Railcar Services name, was repairing a wide range of privately owned stock, and while tank wagons belonging to Algeco, BP, BRTE, Charringtons, Petrofina, Procor, Shell and Total were the most common vehicles to be seen, other types might also be found in the works yard. Among the rarer visitors were these three British Steel Glasgow PAAs, built to carry lime from Hardendale Quarry to Ravenscraig steelworks, which were recorded at Stoke in October 1986.

Although by the early 1970s most power station coal traffic was being carried in Merry-Go-Round hopper wagons, a handful of power stations continued to be served by trains of traditional 16-ton Minerals. The National Coal Board's Hunslet 0-6-0ST 'Spitfire' (works No. HE3831, built 1955) hauls a rake of MGR hoppers into the BR exchange sidings at Bickershaw Colliery, near Leigh, in May 1973. Also in the sidings is another train of MGR hoppers waiting to depart for Fiddlers Ferry power station, while the rake of loaded 16-tonners will leave later that afternoon for Rose Grove from where it would be tripped to either of the local power stations at Huncoat or Padiham.

Coal Traffic On and Off the Merry-Go-Round

For well over four decades Merry-Go-Round trains were a cornerstone of Britain's railfreight industry conveying coal from pit-head and port to power stations in England, Scotland and Wales. Devised in the early 1960s the most significant elements of the MGR operation were the purpose-built 32-ton capacity two-axle hopper wagons, which could be both loaded and unloaded while on the move, so that the trains could pass through the hopper discharge house at a controlled speed and without any need for the consist to be shunted.

Consequently the introduction of MGR working brought much greater efficiency both in the use of locomotives and rolling stock, for not only could BR dispense with the strings of loose-coupled wagons requiring time-consuming marshalling that had previously been employed, but on many of the shorter distance flows between colliery and power station MGR wagon sets were able to accomplish three or even four round trips in a day.

The first MGR train ran from Manton Wood Colliery, near Worksop, to West Burton Power

Station in November 1965 and thereafter MGR workings gradually increased, particularly to the Central Electricity Generating Board's newly commissioned 2,000MW (2GW) baseload power stations that had recently opened, or were under construction, at Cottam, Didcot, Eggborough, Ferrybridge, Fiddlers Ferry, Ratcliffe-on-Soar and West Burton. Additionally, in subsequent years the power stations at Abethaw, Blyth, Drakelow, Ironbridge, Rugeley and Thorpe Marsh would also be equipped to receive MGR trains, as were those at Cockenzie and Longannet operated by the South of Scotland Electricity Board. As a result by 1978 British Rail was delivering more than 61 million tons of coal a year to the CEGB and SSEB.

Until the wholesale colliery closures of the 1990s most coal-fired power stations, including the 2GW stations, drew most if not all of their coal from local collieries. The main exceptions were Didcot, which was served by up to 14 MGR trains a day from the Midlands, and Fiddlers Ferry power station situated north of the River Mersey. Opened in 1971, three miles to the west of Warrington, Fiddlers Ferry received around half its coal from the

handful of surviving collieries in Lancashire, Staffordshire and north Wales, while the rest came from the Yorkshire coalfield, initially via the electrified Woodhead route until that line closed in 1981 when the MGR trains were rerouted via Healey Mills.

However, a major change was heralded in 1989 when BR operated the first trainload of imported coal from Liverpool Gladstone Dock to Fiddlers Ferry and by winter 1992 almost 30% of the power station's coal was arriving from Liverpool (see Fiddlers Ferry coal programme). In the interim, privatisation of the electricity supply industry had seen all of the country's coal-fired power stations sold to either National Power or Powergen, both of whom were keen to diversify their sources of supply, and at Liverpool Docks Powergen would invest £40 million into a purpose-built rapid loading terminal which came into use in August 1993. In addition to supplying Fiddlers Ferry, the new Liverpool Bulk Terminal also despatched MGR trains to other Powergen stations such as Cottam and Ironbridge, while imports of industrial coal also began to be railed from Liverpool to the Castle Cement

During the mid-1980s the MGR trains from Bickershaw and Parkside collieries to Fiddlers Ferry power station were invariably hauled by pairs of Class 20s and Nos. 20158 and 20160 are pictured at Warrington Bank Quay with 6T76, the 12.30 Fiddlers Ferry PS to Parkside, in June 1985. This daily diagram comprised three round trips from Parkside to Fiddlers Ferry as well as a single working from Bickershaw.

By the early 1990s Class 60s had become a regular sight on MGR trains to Fiddlers Ferry and on June 12, 1993 No. 60060 is seen at Crewe with 7F39, the 09.40 from Silverdale Colliery. The two-axle MGR hoppers, TOPS coded HAA, were limited to 45mph when loaded but could run at up to 60mph when empty.

Despite the success of the original MGR operation the newly privatised National Power sought to increase the efficiency of its coal trains still further when in 1994 they ordered six of their own Class 59 locomotives for use on the coal and limestone trains to Drax. Class 59 No. 59105 arrives back at Gascoigne Wood with a rake of empty JMA bogie coal hoppers from Drax power station on July 29, 1997.

Fiddlers Ferry coal train programme for week commencing Sunday, October 11 1992. The 89 planned workings would deliver some 106,200 tonnes of coal to the power station.

With the arrival of EWS's own HTA bogie coal hoppers in 2001, the former National Power JMAs were briefly reallocated to the Liverpool Fiddlers Ferry coal circuit, but by 2004 most were either stored or in aggregate traffic. Still in National Power livery, albeit rather faded, JMA No. NP19630 is pictured at Doveholes Quarry, Peak Forest, in July 2006.

The closure of many deep mines resulted in a significant increase in the movement of opencast coal from Scotland to English power stations. Class 66 No. 66059 leaves the stabling sidings at Milford Junction with 6S18, the 09.58 to Falkland Junction, Ayr, on August 20, 2001. This was one of four such daily empty workings from Milford West Sidings all of which were routed via the Settle and Carlisle. From Ayr the rake of MGR hoppers would go forward as required to either Chalmerston, Killoch, Knockshinnoch or New Cummnock for loading.

The two-axle air-braked 32-ton capacity Merry-Go-Round coal hoppers were one of the most successful wagon types ever built, with 11,161 being constructed at BREL's Ashford, Darlington and Shildon works between 1964 and 1982. HAA No. 353910 was still in its original livery of freight brown for the framing and unpainted body when photographed at Chatterley Valley Opencast Disposal Point in February 1993.

When first designed the MGR hoppers were intended to have a canopy, known as a 'Top Skip', although it was soon found that the full payload of 32 tons of coal was achievable without it. Initially only about 180 had them although more were fitted in the 1990s as it prevented finer coal being 'blown off' particularly on the longer Anglo-Scottish flows. At the same time the 'Top Skip' hoppers were recoded HCA, No. 351168 being recorded at Oakleigh Sidings, Northwich, in July 1994.

works at Clitheroe and Penyffordd.

Meanwhile the local coal originating points had gradually closed as British Coal struggled to sell its output at an economic rate. Both Bickershaw and Parkside collieries, which between them had once despatched up to 10 MGR trains a day to Fiddlers Ferry, closed in 1992 although the colliery at Point of Ayr, to the east of Prestatyn, would continue to load one or two trains a week for Fiddlers Ferry until 1996. The mine at Silverdale, situated to the north west of Stoke-on-Trent, which in its last years was run by Midlands Mining, would finally close in 1998, although by then its occasional trains were running to Didcot. Also in Staffordshire the opencast disposal point at Chatterley Valley, north of Stoke, which had opened in 1988 to supply Fiddlers Ferry, Ironbridge, and Rugeley, was last used in 1999.

It was a similar story around the country for in the aftermath of the year-long miners' strike of 1984 pit closures had been accelerated and in the Yorkshire coalfield alone 27 pits were closed between 1985 and 1996. In place of deep-mined coal the electricity generators were turning to imports and in addition to the new coal loading bunker at Liverpool a similar facility, equipped with two 2,500-tonne overhead silos, was opened at Avonmouth in 1993 by National Power. Avonmouth then became the main source of coal for Didcot, as well as occasionally loading MGR trains for Aberthaw and Rugeley, while on the east coast new workings to the baseload power stations located in Nottinghamshire and Yorkshire were introduced from the docks at Hull, where the government had provided a Section 8 grant for a new pad loading facility, and from Immingham where two new loading pads had been installed alongside the reception sidings. There was also a significant increase in the tonnage of opencast coal being railed across the Scottish border from various loading points in Ayrshire to power stations in England, and in the early 1990s BR spent more than £60 million refurbishing the Settle and Carlisle line to handle these trains on their way to the Aire Valley power stations at Drax,

Eggborough and Ferrybridge.

In 1994 National Power invested in its own fleet of six Class 59 locomotives that were built at the General Motors works in London, Ontario, together with 21 JHA and 85 JMA hopper wagons built by Oy Transtech in Finland. The JHAs were to be used as a block train carrying limestone from Tunstead Quarry, near Buxton, to the newly installed flue-gas desulphurisation plant at Drax power station, while the JMAs would work in sets of 17 wagons, the equivalent of 36 HAAs, carrying coal from the super-pit at Gascoigne Wood, near Selby, to both Drax and Eggborough. The National Power train sets also worked from Maltby Colliery to Drax, but following railfreight privatisation National Power sold its entire rail operation to EWS in April 1998.

In 2004 the Selby coalfield was closed bringing to an end the once intensive schedule of departures from Gascoigne Wood and the former NP Class 59s and JHAs were then redeployed on stone trains from the Mendips and the Peak District, while the JMA hoppers were transferred to Liverpool to the Fiddlers Ferry coal circuit. In later years they would also be reallocated to stone traffic as EWS's new build of HTA bogie coal hoppers began to be delivered.

The prospects for power station coal continued to look rosy in the late 1990s, such that both EWS and Freightliner, and later GBRf and Fastline, all invested in new rolling stock for the traffic. The largest of these new fleets were the 1,145 HTAs built for EWS at the Thrall Wagon Works in York between 2001 and 2004, while Freightliner's initial purchase of 446 HHA bogie coal hoppers was soon followed by an order for 220 HXAs. Subsequently both GBRf and Jarvis Fastline also acquired their own fleets of bogie coal hoppers, many leased from either VTG or General Electric, although following the financial collapse of Jarvis Rail their 94 IIA coal hoppers were transferred to GBRf in 2010.

The year 2010 also saw the last of the HAA MGR coal hoppers taken out of service, but remarkably within less than a decade

most of the HTAs and HHAs had suffered a similar fate. In 2013, amid increasing concerns over climate change, the UK government introduced the top-up carbon tax, a measure intended to encourage the power generators to use greener fuels, and in 2015 the tax was doubled. By 2016 railborne coal traffic had fallen by almost 70% with the power stations at Cockenzie, Didcot, Ferrybridge, Ironbridge, Longannet and Rugeley having all closed, while at Aberthaw, Eggborough and Fiddlers Ferry generating was scaled back. At Fiddlers Ferry the DB Schenker worked trains from Liverpool Dock ceased to run in 2015, as did the twice daily Freightliner-hauled working from Manisty Wharf at Ellesmere Port, and by 2017 the power station was only receiving the occasional coal train from either Portbury or Redcar, as well as a short-term working from the now-closed Ferrybridge conveying stockpiled coal.

However, alongside the decline in coal came the rise of biomass traffic with Drax power station burning its first test load in 2004 and by 2015 three of the six generators at Drax had been converted to run on biomass. The first trainloads ran from Tyne Dock in 2010 and were later followed by workings from the docks at Hull and Immingham, while a new 100,000-tonne biomass storage terminal opened at Liverpool Docks in October 2015 and by 2019 Drax was receiving up to a dozen biomass trains a day. Following its conversion to burn biomass the recommissioned 420MW Lynemouth power station also became a destination for the new traffic, with two or three trains a day running from Tyne Dock.

With the biomass pellets having to be kept dry both DB and GBRf fitted a number of their existing coal hoppers with top covers, but being less dense than coal trainload tonnages were reduced. Therefore, a fleet of 250 new purpose-built covered hoppers were constructed by WH Davis between 2013 and 2016 for the biomass workings to Drax, while in 2018 GBRf purchased 50 new covered hoppers with a payload of 70 tonnes from ARI (Romania) for the trains to Lynemouth.

Both Freightliner Heavy Haul and GBRf also won a share of the Anglo-Scottish coal traffic. On August 19, 2011 Class 66 No. 66596 heads south at Ribblehead under a threatening sky with 6Z68, the 07.22 MX Killoch to Cottam PS, formed of Freightliner's 19.1-metre long HXAs.

Freightliner's first batch of bogie coal hoppers were the 19.6-metre long HHAs which could carry 73.6 tonnes. Built by Wagony Swidnica in Poland they were fitted with LTF (low track force bogies) and other than the underframe were unpainted. No. HHA 370066 slips through Barnetby in the consist of an Immingham to West Burton PS working on July 10, 2002.

Very few of Britain's smaller power stations were equipped to unload MGR coal trains and during the 1970s they were either closed or switched to receiving their coal by road. However, in 1991 British Rail won a contract to supply the power station at Padiham, near Burnley, with coal from the Maryport Opencast Disposal Point in Cumbria and to handle the traffic it leased 70 two-axle PNA open wagons from Tiger Rail. Appropriately sporting Coal sub-sector livery Class 60 No. 60069 'Humphrey Davy' waits as its train is grab unloaded at Padiham in December 1991.

By 2017 the majority of Britain's coal-fired power stations had either closed or else been reduced to peak-time generation only, with the result that railborne coal traffic had declined by almost 70%. One of the consequences of these closures was a short-term flow of stockpiled coal from Ferrybridge to Fiddlers Ferry and Class 66 No. 66552 is seen heading 6M09, the 12.20 from Ferrybridge, out of Winterbutlee Tunnel, south of Walsden on the Calder Valley line in May 2017.

By 2004 most of the Anglo-Scottish power station coal traffic was being conveyed in the new EWS and FLHH bogie hoppers. One such service was 6M69, the 19.49 from Ravenstruther Opencast Disposal Point to Ironbridge, seen here when formed of 18 HTAs passing Acton Bridge behind Class 66 No. 66169 on April 22, 2005.

After 46 years of service the last of the BR-built MGR hoppers were eventually withdrawn in 2010, but such longevity would not befall EWS's 76-tonne capacity bogie HTA hoppers, as the collapse of power station coal traffic in 2015 resulted in well over half of them going into store. Subsequently some 110 HTAs were modified by the removal of the central hopper section, thus making them more suitable for aggregate which is a denser load than coal, but the rest of the 1145-strong fleet was destined for scrap. Fitted with three-piece cast steel bogies, HTA No. 310259 is seen in almost pristine condition at South Milford in August 2001, but just 17 years later it would be cut up by C.F. Booth's at Rotherham.

The bogie coal hoppers operated by both GBRf and Jarvis Fastline were all fitted with LTF bogies and could carry 74.5 tonnes. The Fastline hoppers were leased from General Electric and given an IIA TOPS code to reflect their having 12-digit UIC numbers. IIA No. 37 70 6791 028-3 is seen at Doncaster in an Immingham to Eggborough PS service on November 14, 2012.

For the first biomass workings between Tyne Dock to Drax power station more than 80 bogie coal hoppers were fitted with moveable aluminium roof doors since the load needed to be kept dry. Former Colas Class 60 No. 60096 *'Impetus'* passes Whitley Bridge Junction with 6H70, the 12.19 Tyne Dock to Drax, on June 27, 2019.

The PNAs used on the Maryport to Padiham circuit had all previously been in aggregate traffic with either Foster Yeoman or ARC. The weekly train to Padiham, normally formed of 34 wagons, ran until March 1993 when the power station was finally closed. PNA No. TRL 5462 is seen at Padiham in February 1992.

With biomass a less dense load than coal, since 2013 some 250 specially designed covered hoppers have been built for the traffic by W. H. Davis. At almost 19 metres in length, the new wagons were fitted with four covered hopper bays, two outside the bogies, in order to maximise their carrying capacity to 116 cubic metres. IIA No. 83 70 0698 057-2 is pictured at South Milford in June 2019.

Several batches of MEAs were built, the first painted in railfreight dark grey, while others were turned out in Loadhaul black, Mainline blue, or EWS red livery, although after privatisation they could all be found working together. Mainline MEA No. M391160 is seen at Margam Yard, deep in former Transrail territory, on August 4, 2000 being shunted by Class 08 No. 08994, one of the Class 08s that had been modified with a cut-down cab to work the Burry Port and Gwendraeth Valley line.

At Ketton the Castle Cement works is connected to BR's Manton to Stamford line by a short, privately operated, branch which runs from Meadow Exchange Sidings to cross the River Chater before going under the A6121 Stamford Road and climbing into the works. In 1996 traffic along the branch, which comprised outgoing cement and inbound coal, was handled by the cement company's Thomas Hill 0-6-0DH, works No. TH293V/built 1980, which is pictured waiting to leave the exchange sidings on August 21. Such was the gradient up into the works that only three loaded coal wagons at a time could be delivered, the third wagon in the rake beyond the two MEAs being one of the Tiger PNAs previously used to supply Padiham which BR had by now purchased.

Other industrial coal traffic, such as to cement works, paper mills and steelworks, was also carried where possible in MGR wagons. Class 47 No. 47222 passes Scunthorpe West Junction with 6D80, the 16.50 Scunthorpe Coal Handling Plant to Dinnington Colliery Junction, in October 1983. At the time British Steel's Scunthorpe CHP was receiving up to eight MGR trains a day from the collieries at Dinnington, Silverwood and Wolstanton. Above the line of loaded HAAs can be seen a Class 08 shunting in Scunthorpe Freight Depot, which at the time was still handling a limited amount of domestic coal traffic, although its main activity was as a loading point for cement brought by road from the Rugby Cement works at South Ferriby. The cement was then forwarded via the wagonload network in the PCA wagons to Foxton, Manchester Ardwick, and Stapleford and Sandiacre.

Not all customers had been able to install the necessary discharge gear to unload MGR trains and consequently coal flows to several cement works had been lost during the 1970s. However, following railfreight sectorisation the coal sector sought to regain some of that traffic and a programme to convert more than 600 redundant HAA and HEA hopper wagons into high-sided minerals was undertaken. Recoded MEA the converted wagons were then used to carry coal to the cement works at Clitheroe, Ketton, Penyffordd and Rugby, as well as handling the carrying of export coal traffic, previously still carried in vacuum-braked 21-tonners, to Swansea Dock. Class 66 No.66086 heads through Newport with a rake of empty MEAs returning from Rugby to the Celtic Energy siding at Parc Slip in June 1999.

One cement works at which hopper discharge equipment had been installed in the 1960s was G&T Earle's Hope Works, Derbyshire, which then belonged to the Associated Portland Cement Manufacturers. After several changes of ownership the works is now part of the Breedon Group, while bogie HTA hoppers replaced the two-axle HAA hoppers supplying Hope with its coal in 2010. As the cement works at Hope is connected to the main rail network by a 1½-mile-long privately operated branch, a number of HTA hoppers, modified with buffers and screw couplings to allow haulage by one of the cement works locomotives along the branch, are used on the weekly coal delivery from Cwmbargoed. A short rake of four HTAs await unloading at the coal discharge shed inside Hope cement works in June 2019.

The transfer of domestic coal traffic to the Speedlink network had been planned for May 1984 but due to the ongoing miners' strike this was not accomplished until 1985, by which date the number of rail-served coal depots had fallen from around 350 in 1979 to just 75. This number would continue to decline sharply in subsequent years, although two that would survive into the new Millennium were the JA Smallshaw coal concentration depots (CCDs) at Gobowen, south of Wrexham, and at Shrewsbury. Class 58 No. 58019 heads past Madeley Junction in May 1985 with 7G19, the 07.55 SX Shrewsbury Coton Hill Yard to Bescot Speedlink, its train consisting of 14 empty HEAs from the CCD at Shrewsbury New Yard and two empty BRA air-braked Borails from Hookagate long-welded rail depot. *(©Colour Rail)*

From 1985 BR's fleet of 1,998 HEA 32-ton capacity hoppers was dedicated to domestic coal, although as the traffic continued to decline many would later be rebuilt as MEA mineral wagons. HEA No. 361345, loaded with phurnacite from the Firegold plant at Immingham Dock destined for the Powell Duffryn Fuels CCD at Totton, near Southampton, is pictured at Immingham Reception Sidings in September 1990.

In November 1986 BR introduced a number of dedicated 'Network Coal' services to try and improve its service to the few CCDs that remained, but the country's switch to alternative sources of domestic heating continued at a pace. By 1993 these dedicated trains were handling less than 200,000 tonnes a year and revenue from domestic coal traffic had collapsed from £12.5 million in 1986 to just under £2 million. Unsurprisingly it was decided to withdraw the rail service to all but two coal depots, with those at Preston and West Drayton thenceforth being served by occasional block trains from the washeries at Coedbach, Gwaun-cae-Gurwen, or Onllwyn. A rake of HEAs from Gwaun-cae-Gurwen stands over the hopper pit at Preston Deepdale CCD in August 1994.

The full loads yard at Gwaun-cae-Gurwen washery was still full of wagons in September 1994. However, most were by then in internal use and as such had been repainted green to differentiate them from those still available for main line traffic

Following the creation of the shadow freight franchises Transrail won a contract to move containerised coal on behalf of British Fuels to several freight depots in Scotland, as well as reintroducing rail service to the coal depots at Blackburn, Carlisle and Gobowen, while in 1997 coal traffic returned to Shrewsbury CCD. Class 56 No. 56067 heads an empty Blackburn CC to Killoch Washery working through Carlisle on May 1, 1998.

Containerised coal traffic was given a further boost in 1986 when Cawoods added a rail connection to its container terminal at Ellesmere Port and invested in a fleet of low-deck two-axle air-braked container wagons. These were designed to accommodate a 20ft x 8ft container for the carriage of domestic coal and patent fuels for export to Ireland. The initial Cawoods trains ran from South Wales but in 1987 additional block workings to Ellesmere Port were introduced running from Lynemouth Colliery and the Coal Products Ltd's Firegold Smokeless Fuel plant at Immingham. Class 56 No. 56124 passes Winwick Quay with 6M21, the 09.37 Lynemouth to Ellesmere Port, on August 14, 1992.

In 1984 British Rail was anticipating that the remaining coal depots would be served only by its fleet of HEA air-braked hopper wagons, but during that year agreement was reached with the Scottish distribution company JG Russell for the use of Gartcosh goods yard as a receiving point for coal. Consequently more than 170 redundant air-braked two-axle SAA steel carriers were modified by fitting them with container fixing brackets to enable the carriage of Russell's end-door coal containers. Recoded FPA No. 400141 was recorded passing Crewe Gresty Lane in the consist of 6S75, the 12.55 SX Severn Tunnel Junction to Mossend Speedlink, in June 1985.

The 'Enterprise' wagonload service, introduced by Transrail in 1994, saw a return to rail for the anthracite traffic between the washery at Onllwyn and PD Stirling's distribution depot at Mossend. In 2003 the traffic was switched from HEA hopper wagons into containers and FCA No. 610202, carrying two loaded Celtic Energy open-top containers from Onllwyn, waits to continue its journey north at Warrington Arpley yard in March 2007.

Fortunately when the aggregate industry came calling in the early 1970s BR had a large number of redundant 27-ton MSV ex-iron ore tipplers available for stone traffic. To designate their new use some were adorned with a 'Stone' symbol, as illustrated by this view of Class 52 No. D1013 'Western Ranger' heading through Bedford St John's station with a Westbury to Leagrave block limestone train in July 1975. (©Colour Rail)

Moving Mountains,
Aggregate and Cement on Rail

AGGREGATE

Until the early 1970s the construction industry had largely relied upon conveniently located local sources of stone and other aggregates such as sand and gravel. However, the motorway building programme, coupled with unprecedented investment in commercial and residential property particularly in London and the Home Counties, saw a number of quarrying companies turn to rail to provide them with an economic means of bringing large tonnages of building materials from further afield.

Fortunately wagon availability was not a problem as British Steel had recently begun using its own bogie wagons releasing a substantial fleet of BR 27-ton iron ore tipplers that could be redeployed in aggregate traffic. Furthermore, with the demand for domestic coal falling, increasing numbers of 21-ton coal hoppers were also being set aside. However, both they and the iron ore tipplers wagon were elderly, vacuum-braked, and could only be regarded as a stop-gap until they were replaced by new air-braked hoppers capable of operating at up to 60 mph in block train formations.

First to introduce such wagons were the Mendips-based firms Amalgamated Roadstone (ARC) and Foster Yeoman, who between 1972 and 1974 put into service more than 200 37.5-tonne capacity air-braked PGA hoppers to work from their quarries at Whately and Merehead. However, the aggregate boom was not confined to the Mendips and they were soon followed by Thomas Tilling Construction (Tilcon) who in 1973 purchased a fleet of 33 PGAs to work from Rylstone Quarry, north of Skipton, to its new stone terminals at Hull and Leeds, while in 1974 the Staveley Lime Co. began to forward crushed limestone from Doveholes Quarry at Peak Forest to its Salford Hope St. railhead in a daily block train of 28 PGAs. The former Midland Railway main line through the Peak District would also see trainloads of PGAs begin working from Tarmac's Topley Hill Quarry, near Buxton, to terminals at Pendleton and Widnes.

Bogie stone hoppers became more common during the 1980s and by 1994 they could also be found working from Bardon Hill, Merehead, Peak Forest, Rylstone and Whately. At RMC's Doveholes Quarry, Peak Forest, a fleet of 49 new wagons replaced the earlier PGAs, handling not only the daily working to Salford but also additional services to Bletchley and Washwood Heath. JGA No. RMC17248 was less than a year old when recorded at the quarry in March 1991.

Many of the new privately owned stone hopper wagons introduced during the 1970s and 1980s were painted in colourful and attractive liveries, a marked change to the rather drab colours found on BR's own freight stock. PGA No. PR14033, built by the Standard Wagon Co. of Heywood with English Steel pedestal suspension in 1972 is pictured at Merehead Quarry in April 1981.

Air-braked PGA stone hoppers were introduced in the early 1970s to both the Mendips and Peak District stone workings. Class 37s Nos. 37219 and 37238 head through Guide Bridge with 6J46, the 14.27 from Peak Forest to Salford Hope Street on May 17, 1983. A single set of 37-tonne capacity Peakstone PGAs was able to cover this daily out-and-back working which resulted in a saving in fleet size at the same time as more stone could be delivered per train.

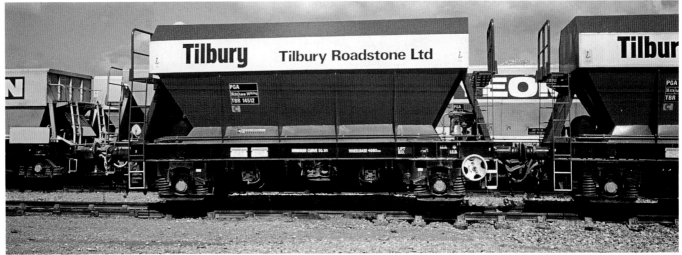

Also recorded at Merehead in April 1981 was PGA No. TBR14512, one of a batch of 23 hoppers built in 1980 to work between Merehead and the Tilbury Roadstone terminal at Barham, near Ipswich. When not required for that job the Tilburys could occasionally be seen running to one of Foster Yeoman's own terminals and like most of the PGAs built from the late 1970s they had their reinforcing ribs on the outside of the hopper body and were fitted with Gloucester pedestal suspension.

A handful of quarries, including those at Bardon, Croft and Caldon Low, continued to employ BR vacuum-braked mineral wagons such as the MSV and MTV into the 1980s, but as the traditional network of wagonload freight service began to be run down their use became increasingly problematic. Such wagons, if needing to be detached en route as a cripple, could be a considerable nuisance to recover while their age made them increasingly prone to failure. A pair of Class 31s prepare to leave the exchange sidings alongside the Leicester to Nuneaton line outside ECC's Croft Quarry with a train of loaded MTVs and MSVs in April 1988, while that same month a line of MSVs, including No. B386175, awaits its next turn of duty at Tarmac's Caldon Low Quarry, which was situated at the end of a freight-only branch from Leek Brook Junction. *(©Trevor Mann collection)*

(©David Ratcliffe)

The ECC quarry at Croft finally switched to loading air-braked hoppers in 1987 when it leased 36 PGAs previously in traffic with ARC. This fleet was then able to cover all of the workings out of Croft supplying each of the stone terminals at Bishops Stortford, Brentford and Bow once or twice a week. PGA No. PR14363 awaits repair at Marcroft Engineering's Stoke in May 1992.

Among the first firms to operate bogie aggregate hoppers was Brett Marine whose fleet of 20 wagons, built by Charles Roberts in 1970, was used to carry sea-dredged sand and gravel from Cliffe in Kent to the company terminals at Purley and Salfords. Recently repainted PHA No. ELC17518 is pictured beneath the rapid loader at Cliffe in April 1993.

to Procor. Refurbished and fitted with ladders and fixed couplings these were then leased to both ARC and Foster Yeoman to supply stone terminals without hopper discharge equipment.

Together with this move towards larger wagons came a change in traction and by 1977 the Westerns, Peaks and Class 47s had been replaced on the Mendip stone trains by Class 56s and pairs of Class 37s. However, their performance on the heavier trains from Merehead proved a disappointment and in December 1985 the first of Foster Yeoman's five new Class 59 locomotives was despatched from General Motors' La Grange works in Chicago, Illinois, arriving by sea at Southampton Docks on January 8, 1986. Fitted with a 3,300 hp turbocharged 16-cylinder engine and 'Super Series Creep' control, to detect and correct wheelslip and thereby improve adhesion and haulage capability, the Class 59s were an immediate success and it was not long before ARC also ordered a fleet of four to haul its trains from Whately. Elsewhere stone traffic remained in the hands of BR locomotives including the 3,100 hp Class 60 first introduced in 1989 of which 31 were initially allocated to the construction sector.

Railfreight privatisation initially had little impact on aggregate traffic, other than for the replacement of the remaining Class 37s and 56s by new EWS Class 66s, but from the late 1990s there has been a steady increase as the new railfreight companies have offered increasingly attractive haulage rates when compared to road. Some existing terminals have been expanded, mothballed terminals reactivated and several new unloading points opened, with many new services being introduced. At the same time the wagon fleet has also been renewed and in recent years large numbers of new 77-tonne capacity open wagons have been introduced by the major railfreight operators, while numerous redundant bogie coal hoppers have been transferred to stone traffic, either in as-built condition or after modification.

Lagging somewhat behind were the Midlands quarries and it was not until 1979 that Redland purchased its first PGAs to handle traffic from the expanded Buddon Wood Quarry at Mountsorrel to terminals in Bedfordshire and East Anglia. In 1986 a fleet of 51 new 68-tonne capacity bogie hoppers began working from Bardon Hill Quarry, near Coalville, to West Drayton, while finally in 1987 a pool of 36 Procor-owned PGAs, no longer required by ARC, took over most of the stone traffic from the ECC quarry at Croft, situated alongside the Leicester to Nuneaton line, to the stone terminals at Brentford and Bow.

With movement costs being such a significant factor in the price of aggregate, it is perhaps a surprise that in the 1970s only three firms, Francis Parker, Murphy Aggregates (Marcon) and Marinex (Brett Marine) had invested in bogie wagons, but at the time such vehicles were considerably more expensive

than four-wheelers, both in terms of initial outlay and in ongoing maintenance costs. However, all three of these companies were able to offset the cost as their wagons were used on short-distance movements, the Marinex and Murphy wagons being able to accomplish two loaded workings a day while the Francis hoppers made up to six daily journeys between the gravel pits at Lavant and a washing plant at Drayton, a journey of no more than six miles from one side of Chichester to the other.

By 1982 aggregate traffic had more than quintupled, from around two million tonnes in 1969 to more than 11 million, and as the decade progressed tonnages continued to rise with new bogie wagons also being built for ARC, Foster Yeoman, RMC (who had acquired the Staveley Lime Co.) and RH Roadstone. In addition the closure of Consett steelworks in 1980 had seen 114 bogie iron ore tipplers sold

The closure of Consett steelworks in 1981 was followed by the sale of the 114 British Steel Teeside PTA air-braked bogie box wagons to Procor. After being fitted with ladders, and having their rotary couplers secured in the fixed position, they were then leased to both Foster Yeoman and ARC replacing the last of the BR-owned MSVs on the workings from Merehead and Whately to stone terminals that were not equipped for hopper discharge such as those at Appleford, Crawley, Fareham, Harlow, Oxford and Purfleet. While unloading times were greater than for an equivalent train of hopper wagons, the use of large mechanical grabs meant they were not prohibitively so, and indeed this method of operation would come to be increasingly popular. All the PTAs were repainted but unlike those leased to Foster Yeoman, where a change of number prefix was deemed sufficient, those leased to ARC were renumbered in the PR26801-50 series. In ARC's eye-catching mustard yellow livery PTA No. PR26823 was recorded at Westbury in September 1991, while PTA No. PR26481 on hire to Yeoman is seen at Merehead Quarry in September 1991.

Within each SDT wagon set one of the PHAs was also fitted with a 65 hp Lister engine to drive the conveyor while each Transfer wagon, of which four were eventually built from former Railease bogie conflats, carried a 100 hp power pack to drive its rotating turret and cantilevered boom. The versatility of the Self-Discharge Trains meant that Redland was able to supply temporary and/or awkward-to-reach locations, as is illustrated in this July 1991 view of one delivering ballast to the newly laid DMU stabling sidings at Aylesbury.

An alternative and innovative approach to delivering stone appeared in 1988 when the Standard Wagon Co. of Heywood, in collaboration with Redland Aggregates, developed the Self-Discharge Train. This combined the advantages of hopper discharge with the flexibility of being able to be unloaded at almost any location. Initially four 10-wagon SDT sets were built with the first seen waiting to leave Heywood for Mountsorrel in March 1988. With the Self-Discharge concept a success a further 80 SDT wagons were built the following year, either as 10 or five-wagon sets since some destinations could only accommodate a 35-wagon train.

Each set of SDT wagons was fitted with a conveyor belt running along its entire length at solebar level, while each of the end wagons in a set was fitted with extendable arms which, when raised, both tensioned the belt and lifted it over that of another SDT set or the conveyor fitted to the Transfer wagon. After the first four 10-wagon SDT sets had been built the design of the hopper wagons and the livery underwent a slight alteration, while their TOPS code was changed from PGA to PHA. The end wagons were also fitted with mesh guards as seen on No. REDA16217 at Mountsorrel in August 1994.

Sand from the Tarmac siding at Marks Tey, on the Great Eastern Main Line, has been a long-standing if intermittent rail traffic running to several different destinations in the Greater London area, including Mile End and Hayes and Harlington. On July 6, 2000 former Coal Sector Class 60 No. 60060 'James Watt' was recorded leaving Marks Tey with 6V79, the 09.42 WFO for West Drayton. In addition to Tarmac's own PGA aggregate hoppers the train also included a number of ZGA 'Gunnells', former Procor PGAs modified with cut-down bodies which had been purchased by BR in the 1990s for use as ballast carriers.

Foster Yeoman and ARC eventually pooled their Class 59 fleets establishing Mendip Rail to jointly manage their rail operations. After running round its train in Westbury station Class 59 No. 59002, named *'Alan J Day'* and repainted in the green and orange Mendip Rail livery, heads past Fairwood Junction with 7V16, the 11.48 Fareham to Merehead, on September 12, 2002.

In the 1980s Class 56s were an increasingly common sight on stone trains, both from the Midlands and Mendips quarries, and on July 12, 1984 No. 56032 *'Sir De Morgannwg/County of South Glamorgan'* was recorded at Botley propelling 6063, the 10.00 from Westbury (ex-Merehead), through the hopper unloading shed. On this occasion the train was formed of 22 Tilbury Roadstone PGAs rather than Foster Yeoman's own hopper wagons.

In 2018 Hanson Aggregates redeveloped the site of the old Kelbit bitumen sidings at Ashton-in-Makerfield into a stone terminal served by a daily train from its quarry at Shap. As the terminal can only be accessed by a kick-back from the stub of the former Wigan to Haydock branch, the loaded train must first run to Tuebrook Sidings, Liverpool, where it is divided to be forwarded in two portions to Ashton-in-Makerfield. Having only recently been purchased by GBRf, and the first of the class to be repainted, Class 60 No. 60095 propels empty JNA wagons on to the remains of the Haydock branch at Ashton-in-Makerfield on October 22, 2018.

Several new stone terminals have also been opened in recent years, including one at the previously disused Warrington Dallam freight depot. Since 2016 this has been the destination for a thrice-weekly block train of limestone from the Peak Forest, seen here being shunted by Class 66 No. 66177 on July 11, 2018.

In 2016 a new rail loading point with three sidings, each able to accommodate up to 10 bogie wagons, was opened alongside the Settle to Carlisle line at Helwith Bridge to serve Tarmac's Arcow and Dry Rigg quarries. The site loads around five trains of gritstone a week, which are destined for either Bredbury, Hull, Hunslet, Pendleton, or Scunthorpe, the gritstone being in great demand for use on motorways either as coated stone or as a top dressing. GBRf's Class 66 No. 66774 shunts JNAs being loaded for Scunthorpe in the sidings at Helwith Bridge on July 3, 2019. The line of yellow posts between sidings one and two form part of the dust-suppression system which was installed to reduce the amount of airborne dust during loading.

LEFT: Several new limestone workings from the Peak District were introduced from the mid-1990s as concerns over acid rain saw the installation of flue-gas desulphurisation plants at a number of coal-fired power stations. Among such trains was 6E56, the 06.40 Tunstead Quarry to Drax, seen here at Doncaster behind Class 66 No. 66606 on July 12, 2006. Freightliner Heavy Haul had recently gained this contract and it was one of the first uses for its fleet of new HIA bogie hoppers.

Following the collapse in the demand for power station coal both DB and GBRf embarked on a programme to modify some of their coal hoppers for stone traffic. The higher density of aggregate meant that the wagons could be shortened by removing the central bays without reducing the payload each could carry, this in turn enabling more wagons per train. DB renumbered and recoded its modified HTAs to HRAs, as illustrated by the recently completed HRA No. 41 70 6723 005-8 recorded passing Crewe Basford Hall in April 2018.

Initially GBRf's shortened ex-coal hoppers were left unpainted but in summer 2019 a new white livery featuring VTG, GBRf and Cemex lettering was introduced for wagons newly modified and intended to work out of Cemex's Dove Holes limestone quarry at Peak Forest. HYA 371023 is pictured at Peak Forest in July 2019.

More than 500 new 101.6-tonne glw bogie open box wagons were imported into Britain during 2016/17. Built at Greenbrier's Astra Rail works in Romania they were fitted with Low Track Force bogies and had a capacity of 77 tonnes, with the first batches appearing in either Ermewa grey or VTG blue livery, although some also had Mendip Rail or Tarmac lettering. Most went immediately into aggregate traffic but one batch of VTG-owned JNAs leased to DB was also used to carry gypsum, colliery spoil and sand. VTG's JNA No. 81 70 5500 336-9 is pictured at Hellifield when on its way back from the British Gypsum works at Newbiggin in August 2018.

BELOW: The Ermewa-owned JNAs were similar to those built for VTG but had only nine vertical reinforcing bodyside ribs. Complete with a Tarmac logo No. 81 70 5500 024-1 was recorded at Hyde North when en route from Mountsorrel to Ashbury stone terminal on August 20, 2019. This was another new working that had been introduced earlier in the year.

Among the new 77-tonne capacity open box wagons were batches from each of the three largest freight operating companies but unlike the JNAs from Ermewa and VTG those introduced by GBRf, in common with DB's MMAs, were fitted with a door in each side to facilitate cleaning out the interior. JNA No. 81 70 5500 458-1 was loaded with gritstone for Scunthorpe when photographed at Arcow Quarry, Helwith Bridge, in July 2019.

Freightliner's equivalent bogie box wagons, coded MWA, differ still further with their side doors positioned in one of the end panels while many were built using bogies and brake gear recovered from the company's withdrawn HHA coal hoppers. The first batch of 64 MWAs was delivered in Freightliner green livery but the second batch, numbering 76, is painted in the Genesee and Wyoming-inspired grey and orange scheme, G&W having acquired Freightliner in 2015. When almost new MWA No. 81 70 5891 570-0 was recorded passing Peak Forest en route to Tunstead Quarry in July 2019.

While most railborne cement was transported in bulk in block trains until the early 1980s there was also some rail movement of bagged cement to smaller depots via the wagonload network, and Class 25 No. 25327 waits to leave Truro with two APCM Palvans forming the 15.00 trip to Chacewater on June 30, 1975. Between 1964 and 1966 the Standard Wagon Co. of Heywood had built 96 two-axle vacuum-braked 22.5t Palvans for the Associated Portland Cement Manufacturers, which were 25ft 6in over headstocks, with a 16ft wheelbase, and had a similar split sliding door arrangement as the BR Vanwides providing a 9ft-wide opening. However, the ends of the APCM vans were plywood reinforced with upright T-stanchions and diagonal L-angles and they were fitted with roller bearing from new. They were used to carry bags of special cements, such as Snowcrete and Walcrete, from the APCM works at Snodland and Swanscombe in Kent and could be seen working to Blue Circle Cement depots across the country. *(©Trevor Mann Collection)*

CEMENT

Railborne cement has had a more chequered history than aggregates, enjoying a boom in the 1960s and 1970s when the very successful British Railways-designed 22-ton capacity Presflo wagon helped rail establish a strong position. Like the major quarrying companies many of the larger cement firms would also then go on to invest in their own rolling stock and by the early 1980s there were almost 2,000 bulk cement wagons in service on BR. However, growing competition from cheaper foreign imports would then lead to a gradual rationalisation within the domestic cement industry, resulting in the closure of many of the smaller works and rail-served terminals. By 1992 Rugby Cement had ceased to use rail entirely and Blue Circle was loading rail traffic only at Dunbar (Oxwellmains) and Hope, while cement traffic from three of the Castle Cement Group works, at Clitheroe, Penyffordd, and Tring, had also ended leaving just the daily service from the Castle's Ketton works to Kings Cross still running.

Fortunately since the turn of the century cement traffic has picked up and in 2003 block trains began running from a new cement plant at Tunstead to Hunslet, West Thurrock and Willesden, while that same year a working from La Farge's Westbury

Railfreight customers along the Fylde line west of Preston were served by 7P87, the 10.43 Warrington Walton Old Junction to Burn Naze, near Fleetwood, which also called as required en route at Salwick and Kirkham and Wesham. By 1984 traffic from ICI's Hillhouse Works at Burn Naze was minimal, while BNFL's Springfield Works at Salwick received no more than two or three tank wagons each week, but there were still regular deliveries of cement to the small Blue Circle Cement terminal at Kirkham and Wesham. On August 24 Class 40 No. 40182 had four loaded 'depressed-centre' PCAs for Kirkham in tow when photographed heading north at Wigan North Western.

In 1984 a new wagon design, the 'Metalair', was developed, which although of similar capacity to earlier PCAs was cheaper to build. As with the 'depressed-centre' PCAs Blue Circle invested heavily in the new type purchasing more than 180 of which a few were delivered in full BCC livery rather than in the more common plain grey. PCA No. BCC11014 is seen at Earles Sidings, Hope, in June 2001.

Until the 1970s the British Rail Presflo wagons had been in widespread use for carrying cement, but they were then gradually replaced by new air-braked designs, the most numerous of these being the 38-tonne capacity 'depressed-centre' PCAs which were operated by both Blue Circle and Ketton. An unusually clean Ketton PCA, No. TRL9463, is pictured at Bletchley in July 1979.

Bulk cement has long been big business for BR, ever since the introduction of the 22-ton capacity vacuum-braked Presflo bulk powder wagon, of which more than 1900 were built between 1954 and 1964. Consequently they became a common sight at most of the cement works across the country, although by the 1980s their numbers had dwindled as new air-braked powder wagons replaced them on most cement workings. The last BR Presflos in service ran from the Tunnel Cement Co. Padeswood Works at Penyffordd, near Wrexham, to a terminal at Leeds Whitehall Road freight depot until they were finally withdrawn in 1984. Presflo PCV No. B887837 is pictured awaiting cutting up at Liverpool Spekeland Road in August 1986.

cement works to Southampton was also introduced. This involved the use of new KAA 'Piggyback' wagons, carrying both bulk cement tankers and curtain-sided road trailers, but unfortunately after only a few months it was withdrawn. Rather more successfully in 2008 a new thrice-weekly working from Clitheroe to Scotland was introduced, reviving a traffic flow that had ceased in 1992, while that same year also saw the opening of a new terminal at West Thurrock which was supplied from both Hope and Tunstead. In more recent years cement ladings have continued to grow with the addition of an almost daily Clitheroe to Avonmouth working beginning in 2016, while in 2017 the works at Hope, now owned by Hope Construction Materials, began supplying a new terminal at Dagenham. All these new flows benefitted from the introduction of new bogie wagons as did the continuing workings from Oxwellmains to the terminals at Aberdeen, Inverness, Seaham and Uddingston.

ABOVE RIGHT AND RIGHT: Despite earlier setbacks with intermodal wagons the Strategic Rail Authority remained keen to promote innovative wagon designs and in 2002 part-funded a fleet of 22 'Mega-3 Piggyback' wagons, so named as they could carry road trailers, swap-bodies, or containers, which were built by Babcock Rail. Numbered BCC 11501-22, and coded KAA, the 'Mega-3s' were 56ft long and capable of 75mph running on their Y33 bogies carrying a payload of 38.2 tonnes. The production batch entered service in 2003, with six joining an earlier prototype on a new working from Hope Cement Works to Selby, while the other 16 formed a block train running from Westbury Cement Works to Southampton Millbrook container terminal. The Southampton train conveyed bulk cement tankers newly built by Feldbinder, while the Selby service was a mix of Feldbinder bulk tankers and new Boalloy curtain-sided trailers which were loaded with bagged cement. On June 20, 2003 Sentinel 0-6-0DH (works No. RR10221) heads a rake of the new wagons at Westbury cement works while KAA No. BCC11504 is pictured beneath one of the loading silos at Westbury that same day.

The curtain-sided trailers carried bagged cement but their small size told against them and they were stored after only a few months. KAA Nos. BCC11518 and BCC11519 were spotted at Earles Sidings, Hope, in July 2003. All of the KAAs also subsequently went into store until 2007 when 11 were leased by Victa Rail for a new Purfleet to Grangemouth container service. Once again this use proved short-lived and in 2008, after being renumbered and recoded, all 23 'Meg-3s' were despatched, via the Channel Tunnel, to the continent.

Built by Feldbinder in 2008 originally for hire to La Farge, No. VTG12403 was one of several JPAs to have been transferred to Tarmac when spotted at Crewe on May 23, 2018 when returning empty from Willesden to the Tarmac works at Tunstead.

In 2018 GBRf took over the cement workings from Clitheroe and on August 10 Class 66 No. 66716 is pictured passing through Hellifield with 6S00, the 17.05 Clitheroe to Mossend formed of a dozen Feldbinder-built JPAs.

More successful than the 'Meg-3s' was the pool of 16 bogie Cargowaggon vans that were repainted in Blue Circle livery in 1999 for bagged cement traffic from Hope to Moorswater. IPA No. 33 80 2797 611-1 is pictured at Moorswater in June 2001.

While the 'piggyback' wagons proved to be unsuccessful in cement traffic, the next two decades saw considerable investment in new bogie bulk cement wagons by Castle Cement, La Farge, Tarmac and Hope Construction Materials. JPA No. 81 70 9316 039-5, photographed at Earles Sidings in June 2018, is one of 48 82-tonne capacity bogie cement wagons built by Feldbinder in 2016 to work from HCM's Hope Works to Dagenham and Theale.

In addition to being used for construction, limestone is also required by the chemical industry for the production of soda ash (sodium carbonate), a compound used extensively by both the glass and detergent industries. At the end of the 1930s new block workings, using purpose-built bogie hopper wagons, were introduced from ICI's Tunstead Quarry, near Buxton, to its chemical plants at Northwich located at the heart of the Cheshire saltfield. Initially the trains were hauled by LMS 8F 2-8-0 locomotives with diesel power in the form of Sulzer Type 2s taking over in 1963. By 1984 the trains were in the hands of double-headed Class 20s and Nos. 20185 and 20077 coast through Chinley with 6F42, the 13.15 Tunstead to Lostock Works, Northwich, in May of that year.

Following the break-up of the ICI empire in 2000 the soda ash business had been sold off with the new owners adopting the name Brunner Mond Ltd. Consequently the fleet of 27 new 76-tonne capacity bogie hoppers, coded JEA, were delivered with BM lettering as seen in this view of No. BM19712 recorded at Peak Forest in July 2018.

A total of 152 vacuum-braked bogie 43½-tonne capacity hoppers were purchased by ICI between 1936 and 1953 and they remained in traffic until 1997. PHV No. ICIM19148, built in 1953, is pictured at Oakleigh Sidings, Northwich, in April 1994.

BELOW: After briefly using second-hand two-axle aggregate hoppers on the Tunstead to Northwich service, a new fleet of air-braked bogie hoppers was introduced in 2000. Class 60 No. 60059 rounds the curve at Peak Forest with 6F05, the 16.10 Tunstead to Lostock Works, on July 25, 2018. By this date only one of the former ICI chemical works in Northwich continued to produce soda ash and the service from Tunstead had been reduced from four to just one train a day.

Class 37 No. 37259 waits to leave Pendleton Amasco Sdgs. with 6H34, the 09.42 departure for Peak Forest South, in late spring 1983. The train is comprised entirely of Tarmac-owned PGA wagons from a batch of 22 built by the Standard Wagon Co. in 1979. (©Trevor Mann collection)

Stone Traffic to Pendleton

The success of the air-braked stone trains out of the Mendips, on behalf of Amalgamated Roadstone and Foster Yeoman, encouraged other aggregate companies to use rail and in 1977 Tarmac obtained a Section 8 grant in order to introduce a similar operation from its quarry at Topley Pike, situated on the freight-only line between Peak Forest and Buxton, to terminals at Pendleton and Widnes. In addition to purchasing a fleet of PGA two-axle hopper wagons, Tarmac also refurbished the former Amalgamated Asphalt Co. sidings at Pendleton, Salford, which had fallen into disuse during the 1960s, extending them and installing hopper discharge unloading equipment.

Initially Tarmac's Pendleton terminal, shown in the working timetable as Pendleton Amasco Sdgs., was served by a thrice-weekly train from Topley Pike, but by 1980 there were also two trains a week scheduled to run from the ICI quarry at Tunstead, just south of Peak Forest.

However, with the economic recession of the early-1980s these workings declined and stone traffic to Pendleton ended in 1984. Fortunately the site was not redeveloped and in 2001, when railborne aggregate traffic had begun to experience another boom, its two sidings could easily be brought back into use. With the quarry at Topley Pike having closed in the intervening years the revived service to Pendleton ran from Tunstead, and as Tarmac's fleet of two-axle air-braked hopper wagons was also long gone this booked daily working was formed of Buxton Lime Industries bogie JGA hoppers, subsequently sold to VTG and later supplemented by former RMC JGAs that EWS had purchased in 2007.

From 2016 Pendleton stone terminal also became the destination for regular deliveries of gritstone. Hauled by GBRf the gritstone trains originate from the relaid Arcow Quarry sidings at Helwith Bridge, alongside the Settle to Carlisle line, and in spring 2019 there were normally one or two such trains a week, with these being formed of former HYA and IIA coal hoppers, some of which had been shortened to make them more suitable for stone traffic. Haulage of the Tunstead working switched from DB Schenker to Freightliner during 2016, but DB traction still puts in the odd appearance at Pendleton providing the power for the occasional trainloads of granite that began arriving from Mountsorrel in 2019.

STONE TRAINS AT PENDLETON AMASCO SIDINGS

MAY 1983

6J44 arr. 07.00 TThFO from Topley Pike/MWO from Tunstead

6H34 dep. 09.42 SX to Peak Forest South Sidings

AUGUST 2019

6J44 arr. 01.48 SX from Tunstead

6H43 dep. 07.17 SX to Tunstead

6M37 arr. 18.28 Q from Arcow Quarry

6E39 dep. 22.58 Q to Doncaster Hexthorpe Yard

6M18 arr. 05.44 Q from Mountsorrel

4F01 dep. 10.46 Q to Mountsorrel or Toton Yard

NOTES TO AUGUST ENTRIES:
1. While booked to run each weekday the train from Tunstead normally runs four days a week.
2. 'Q' Freight workings run as required with the Arcow to Pendleton train usually running only on a Wednesday.
3. The working from Mountsorrel to Pendleton, which commenced in spring 2019, usually runs fortnightly.

Prior to their sale to VTG in 2009 the Buxton Lime Industries PGAs had sported a rather attractive blue and white livery with blue lettering, but VTG had them repainted in an overall cream colour with black lettering as carried by No. VTG19203 photographed at Salford Central in June 2015.

In addition to serving its terminal at Pendleton, Tarmac's Standard Wagon-built PGAs were also used to supply the stone terminal at Carterhouse Junction, Widnes, but when planning permission to expand Topley Pike quarry was refused in 1987 the wagons went into store before being scrapped. Fitted with Gloucester pedestal suspension and having a capacity of 38.5 tonnes, PGA No. TAMC14908 is pictured in store at Stoke Wagon Works in April 1990.

Ermewa-owned HOA bogie hoppers, on hire to Tarmac, have also appeared on the Mountsorrel to Pendleton working and No. 81 70 6957 042-9 is pictured passing through Salford Central on September 5, 2019.

RIGHT: Since the stone traffic to Pendleton restarted in 2001 bogie hopper wagons have been used on all services. Class 60 No. 60039 slips through Salford Central with a rake of VTG (ex-Buxton Lime Industries) JGAs forming the retimed 6H43, 11.10 Pendleton Amasco Sidings to Tunstead, on June 11, 2015.

BELOW: Class 66 No. 66006 heads east through Salford Central with 4F01, the 10.46 Pendleton to Mountsorrel, on August 15, 2019. The inbound loaded working had been introduced earlier in the year conveying granite from Mountsorrel and on this occasion the train comprised a set of HJA (ex-National Power) hopper wagons that were acquired by EWS in 1998.

CHAPTER 13

Going Private

Class 47 No. 47100 passes Guide Bridge with Trip 82, the 07.30 Ashburys to Peak Forest and Hindlow, in April 1981. The 16-ton Mineral immediately behind the locomotive was on its way to Buxton coal depot while the following raft of seven BR Prestwins was in granulated limestone traffic from the Steetley quarry at Hindlow. A pool of 28 Prestwins was allocated to Hindlow, the granulated limestone being railed to the United Glass Co. works at Alloa, Glasgow Shettleston and Harlow. Also in the lengthy consist were a number of empty Covhops, sheeted Hoppers and five-plank Opens heading for the ICI works at Hindlow or Tunstead.

In addition to opens and vans for general merchandise traffic British Rail also constructed a number of more specialist wagon types. These included the Presflo and the Prestwin, both of which were intended for the carriage of powdered commodities that were difficult to unload from a standard Covered Hopper, and the Clay Hoods designed to protect the china clay load from the elements. However, by the 1970s BR's rolling stock procurement policy had changed and, while continuing to meet the needs of the nationalised industries and the Armed Forces, they had begun to encourage private sector companies to invest in their own rolling stock. Some railfreight customers did so but others hung on until the early 1980s, when the BR wagons they were still using were either life-expired or, being vacuum-braked, incompatible with BR's plans for an air-braked railway. Notification from BR that those wagons would be withdrawn left such customers with the choice of transferring their traffic to road, or purchasing or leasing their own vehicles.

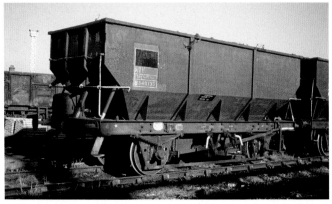

With so many scrapyards scattered around the country scrap metal proved to be a difficult commodity to switch into air-braked wagons. In 1984 Railease, the Standard Wagon Co.'s leasing arm, introduced a fleet of 181 high-sided 35-tonne capacity opens to serve the British Steel electric-arc furnaces at Aldwarke and Deepcar, but the scrap traffic to Allied Steel and Wire in Cardiff would continue to be conveyed in BR 21-ton Minerals and Hoppers until 1987 when Standard Wagon built a new batch of air-braked POA opens. Rebodied BR 21-ton coal hopper HTV No. B340133 awaits loading with steel scrap at Manchester's Ardwick West FD in December 1986, while POA No. RLS4576 is seen outside AS&W's Cardiff Tremorfa Works in August 1991.

The Railease POAs would themselves soon be replaced in the scrap traffic from Manchester to Cardiff by a pool of bogie Tiphook JRAs including No. 33 70 6790 051-0, seen being loaded at Norton's scrapyard in Trafford Park on October 12, 1994.

Of course not all the freight previously carried in unfitted or vacuum-braked wagons was retained on rail. Imported sulphur had been carried in 24-ton iron ore hoppers from Mostyn Dock to the Associated Octel chemical plant at Amlwch on Anglesey, where the sulphur was used in the extraction of bromine from seawater, but with the withdrawal of the hoppers Associated Octel switched to receiving road tanker deliveries of liquid sulphur from Runcorn. HJV No. B439742 is seen at Warrington Walton Old Junction yard in November 1989 shortly after the sulphur traffic had ended. This wagon is now preserved at the Ribble Rail site in Preston.

Closure of Irlam steelworks in the 1970s had seen rail tonnages from Hindlow fall considerably and with Steetley reluctant to fund new wagons the remaining traffic was in danger of switching to road. When the Prestwins were withdrawn in 1983 the movement to Harlow was lost but the Scottish traffic remained on rail courtesy of PD Stirling, the operator of a rail-served distribution depot at Mossend who leased a pool of 10 air-braked Covered Hoppers from Procor. These reached Mossend via Speedlink from where the limestone was roaded to the glassworks in Alloa and Shettleston. PAB No. PR 8015 was recorded at Ashburys on its way back from Mossend to Hindlow in July 1984.

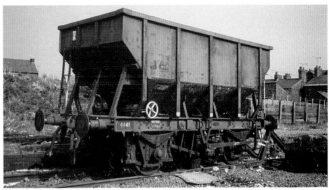

Even when privately owned rolling was available the switch over was not always straightforward, particularly with seasonal traffic such as the movement of rock salt from Over and Wharton in Cheshire. When the BR five-plank opens previously used were withdrawn in the early 1980s it would again be PD Stirling that stepped in, leasing a pool of 12 PSA air-braked opens and 33 PGA air-braked hoppers to carry the salt to receiving points at Inverness, Keith and Mossend, with PSA No. PR25518 being among a mixed rake seen heading north at Warrington Bank Quay in November 1983. However, the economics of leasing vehicles for this temporary traffic proved questionable and the rock salt, which was used to treat icy roads, would be back in BR iron ore tipplers and hopper wagons by 1986, HKV No. B437969 being spotted at Over and Wharton in February 1989.

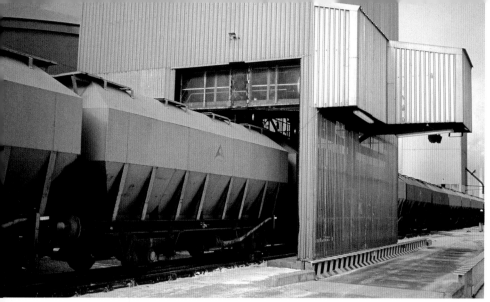

ABOVE AND BELOW: On the Northumberland coast the Alcan aluminium smelter at Lynemouth continued to be supplied with imported alumina carried in unfitted PAO covered hopper wagons until 1994 when they were finally replaced by a pool of second-hand refurbished PCAs previously used to carry either cement or sodium tripolyphosphate. A rake of unfitted alumina covhops, including PAO No. ALCN12026, passes through the loading house at North Blyth in March 1991, while one of the replacement PCAs, No. ALCN11223 was recorded at Blyth in July 2003. The depressed-centre PCAs would remain in service from North Blyth until the smelter at Lynemouth was closed in 2012.

To carry low-level radioactive waste British Nuclear Fuels Ltd. purchased 30 two-axle OBA open wagons from BR which were then modified by having their sides removed and a new stainless steel floor with skip locating brackets fitted. All were recoded and renumbered into the private owner series with PFA No. BNFL91014, loaded with one of the covered skips, being recorded at Sellafield in October 1993. (David Ratcliffe collection)

By the 1980s the need to modernise the wagon fleet also extended to some privately owned fleets still formed of either unfitted or vacuum-braked stock, but two customers, Tioxide and Alcan, whose trains were confined to running over freight-only lines, were able to continue using unfitted wagons into the 1990s. The movement of imported ilmenite ore from Immingham Dock to the Tioxide (previously British Titan Products) works at Grimsby was routed via the Immingham Light Railway and so Tioxide's fleet of 50 29-tonne and 200 32-tonne unfitted Tippler wagons remained in service until 1995 when the traffic was finally transferred to road. TOPS coded PSO No. BTP24539 awaits emptying at the No.4 tippler inside Tioxide's Pyewipe Works in March 1991.

Although there had been some success in persuading customers to invest in their own wagons, when the BR fleet of wooden-bodied Clay Hoods, used to carry china clay and ball clay from the various dries in Cornwall and Devon to Fowey Docks, became due for withdrawal in 1988, English China Clay showed no inclination to fund replacements. However, as the china clay traffic formed a major part of railfreight activity in the West Country, BR reversed its usual policy and built a fleet of 138 CDA covered hoppers between 1988 and 1990. They were based on a prototype converted from an MGR coal hopper fitted with a roller-top cover to protect the clay from the elements. Incorrectly coded as an OOV, UCV No. B743755 is pictured at St Blazey in September 1987, while one of the replacement CDAs No. 375080 is seen at Pontsmill Siding in June 2001.

In 1983 the movement of low-level radioactive waste items, such as clothing and tools, from the BNFL reprocessing plant at Sellafield to the depository at Drigg, was transferred from road to rail with a trip making the short four-mile journey along the Cumbrian coastline most weekdays. Class 25 No. 25285 leaves the British Nuclear Fuels siding at Drigg with 6T60, the 17.00 return working for Sellafield, formed of PFA wagons, on July 31, 1985. *(©Paul Shannon)*

During the 1990s Direct Rail Services, a BNFL subsidiary, gradually took over the operation of all freight traffic into and out of Sellafield, with the low-level waste trip to Drigg becoming a DRS working in 1996. With the waste now being carried in containers the former OBA wagons were replaced by a mixed fleet of two-axle and bogie conflats acquired second-hand by DRS, which included three former Railease 56ft-long bogie conflats originally built in 1983 as part of a 17-strong batch designed to carry containers of potash from Boulby to Severnside. Repainted and re-prefixed BNFL95475 was en route to Drigg when photographed at Seascale in March 2005.

Class 31 No. 31118 leaves Severn Tunnel Junction Up Yard on September 27, 1985 with 6A44, the 09.20 Margam to Swindon, formed of various bogie and two-axle vacuum-braked coil carriers. *(©Trevor Mann collection)*

Modernising the Metals Fleet

Most metals traffic, such as steel bars, rods, ingots, pipes and sections, was carried in open wagons or, for lengthier items, on Bogie Bolsters, but in the 1960s the rising demand for motor vehicles and domestic appliances saw a concomitant increase in the movement of CRC (cold reduced coil). Also known as 'bright steel' cold reduced coil required protection from the elements and initially BR converted a number of existing vehicle types for this traffic, fitting them with cradles and sideways-folding hoods, although as most were vacuum-braked by the early 1980s they were becoming life-expired with

the traffic increasingly switching to road. Consequently in 1986 the south Wales-based wagon builder Powell Duffryn introduced a batch of 55 air-braked covered coil carriers fitted with a one-piece sliding hood and they were immediately put to work on the CRC workings from the steelworks at Llanwern and Port Talbot, supplying steel stockholders in the West Midlands and north of England as well as the British Leyland car body pressing plant at Swindon. Subsequently British Steel had some of its own air-braked iron ore tipplers converted into coil wagons, while among the first new vehicles ordered by EWS was a

batch of telescopic-hood coil carriers. For its other metals traffic British Rail refurbished and updated its existing fleet of Bogie Bolster wagons and in the 1970s fitted 164 vacuum-braked Bogie Bolster Cs with a through air-pipe, while more significantly 1,251 unfitted Bogie Bolster Ds were rebuilt with air brakes and new Y25C or 'Outreau APO 22Y' bogies. In the early 1970s British Rail also introduced almost 1000 new BAA and BBA steel carriers which featured high reinforced ends and a deck made up of transverse 'U' channel section and reinforcing mesh to ensure rapid heat dissipation when loaded with hot steel products.

Among the first vehicles converted for the 'bright steel' coil traffic from south Wales were 20 vacuum-braked bogie slab wagons built in 1961 which were modified in 1966 with new bodywork and sideways-folding hoods. At the same time they were additionally fitted with air brakes and a handful of these dual-braked wagons were still in coil service between Hamworthy and Swindon as late as 1991. Known as 'Coil Ks' they were first allocated the TOPS code JKX which was later altered to BNX. Recently refurbished No. B949550 was photographed at Cardiff Tidal Sidings in August 1991.

In addition to working from Llanwern and Port Talbot the Powell Duffryn coil hoods also replaced BR wagons in carrying imported cold reduced coil from the Poole Harbour Commissioners' siding at Hamworthy to Swindon. The six PXAs leased to J. Carter for this movement had additional 'JOHN CARTER (Poole) LTD' lettering on the hoods, as seen in this view of No. PDUF3025 recorded at Cardiff Tidal Sidings in August 1991. The maximum individual coil weight that could be carried by these wagons was 25 tonnes with a total of six coils able to be accommodated up to the wagons' 74-tonne overall payload.

The movement of 'bright steel' was a lucrative traffic and following railfreight privatisation EWS introduced a fleet of 260 new telescopic-hood BYA coil carriers such as No. 996158, seen at the head of a line of the new wagons alongside a rake of IHA Tiphook (ex-VTG) ferry-fitted sliding-hood wagons inside Shotton steelworks in July 1999. The BYAs were waiting to be loaded with coated coil for the Round Oak steel terminal at Brierley Hill, while the IHAs were at Shotton to collect galvanised coil destined for customers in Germany and Austria.

Another air-braked covered coil carrier to appear in Britain was the short wheelbase, 67-tonne capacity, bogie IHA, which first arrived in 1994, first for cross-Channel traffic but in recent years they have also seen widespread use on domestic coil flows. Both French and Dutch-registered examples were introduced working from south Wales to customers in the Midlands and the north of England as well as on the continent. French-registered IHA No. 31 87 4667 035-1 is seen at the Gilbraith (formerly Fogarty) distribution depot in Blackburn on April 17, 1994.

In line with then current policy, replacement air-braked wagons for the carriage of hot steel products were introduced in the 1970s when BR built 305 BAAs and 551 BBAs. At 40ft over headstocks the BAAs were some 10ft shorter than the BBAs but both were used to carry a range of semi-finished steel items including billets, blooms and slabs. Some were also used to carry hot rolled coil for which many were fitted with cradles so that the coils could be carried on the roll and could therefore be unloaded by a crane hook. BAA No. 900191 is pictured at Immingham Reception Sidings in March 1988, where it had been stopped so that the coil furthest from the camera, which had begun to unravel, could be removed.

The Bogie Bolster C had originally been a GWR design that could carry 30 tons. In the 1970s 164 BR-built examples were fitted with a through air-pipe with the intention that they could then be conveyed in Speedlink services, but in the event most were used in block train workings such as the movement of coated pipes from Leith South FD to selected railheads from where they would be roaded to Gas Corporation work sites. Coded BTW Bogie Bolster C No. B923148 waits to leave Leith in May 1993.

Steel coil that was heading to the finishing plants at Ebbw Vale, Gartcosh, Shotton and Trostre for galvanising or tinplating, was usually loaded hot and could be carried uncovered. Until the 1980s unfitted and vacuum-braked wagons, including the versatile Bogie Bolsters and Boplates, were a common sight in this traffic and Boplate-E No. B947384, together with a Bogie Bolster-D, slips through Newport loaded with steel coil for Shotton in February 1974. *(©John Edser)*

The Bogie Bolster Ds had a payload of 42 tonnes and could be seen loaded with a wide range of items. A rake of BDAs loaded with steel slabs destined for Lackenby are pictured being shunted at Sheffield's Tinsley Yard in June 1986, while BDA No. 950314 was en route from the Bromford Bridge Tube Works to Inverness when recorded at Walton Old Junction Yard, Warrington, in May 1987.

The oil crisis of 1973 resulted in a fall in the demand for heavy fuel oil and many lagged bogie class B tank wagons were rebranded to carry 'Gas Oil or Kerosene Only'. With five such tanks at the front of the formation, Class 40 No. 40177 heads 6M54, the 10.15 SX Leeds to Stanlow Shell company train, past the Wagon Repairs Storrs Hill works at Horbury on April 4, 1977. The outbound workings from Stanlow to Leeds would also include tank wagons of motor spirit and diesel. *(©Trevor Mann collection)*

Tank Trains in Retreat

During the 1960s rising car ownership and the growth in air travel produced a considerable increase in the demand for oil and by the end of the decade British Rail had signed long-term contracts with all the major refiners, and from carrying less than five million tons per annum in 1961, by 1970 more than 18 million tons of petroleum products were being moved by rail.

As part of these contracts the oil companies agreed to modernise their obsolete wagon fleets to take advantage of the increased axleload which had been raised to 22½ tons and soon 45-ton glw two-axle had become the norm. Furthermore, the oil companies began to build oil depots and rebuild existing ones in order to handle trains of up to 2,000 gross tons and by 1966 more

than 200 block petroleum trains were running a week from refineries and coastal tank farms to inland distribution depots and company sidings across the country. That same year a 25-ton axleload was first permitted for trainload operations over specified routes which saw the introduction of the 100-ton glw bogie tank wagon capable of carrying payloads in excess of 70 tons.

Oil traffic peaked at 21.6 million tons in 1972 but thereafter went into a slow but steady decline and had fallen back to 12.3 million tons by 1981. Several factors outside of the railways' control were behind this decline, including the switch to North Sea gas, which reduced the demand for naphtha and LPG (liquid petroleum gas), and the oil crises of 1973 and 1979 which resulted in a considerable fall in the demand for fuel oil. The growing use of pipelines, more exchange agreements between producers, and the closure of many regional distribution terminals in favour of direct road deliveries from refinery to customer, were also to have a significant effect on railborne tonnages.

In the 1970s Shell, with approximately 23% of Britain's refining capacity, had loaded oil trains at its Ardrossan, Shellhaven, Stanlow and Teesport refineries to serve depots situated throughout the country from Connel Ferry and Culloden Moor in the north to Canterbury and Plymouth in the south. However, both Teesport and the small refinery at Ardrossan Harbour, which in its later years had specialised in bitumen production, closed in the mid-1980s, and while Shellhaven would

Until the 1990s Shell Mex and British Petroleum were forwarding about 50% of all railborne petroleum traffic and on May 16, 1989 a pair of Class 47s head east through Manchester Victoria with 6E46, the 07.09 Stanlow to Jarrow company service. Weighing almost 2000 tonnes this train normally ran six days a week and as usual it included both Class A tanks carrying motor spirit and Class B tanks loaded with fuel oil.

Class 85 No. 85020 leans to the curve through Oxenholme with 7M59, the 22.15 MWFO Bishopbriggs to Stanlow service, on October 4, 1978. This working came to an end in 1984 after a pool of 18 bogie Shell tank wagons were reallocated to serve the depot at Bishopbriggs from BP's Grangemouth refinery.

Oil traffic from the Esso refinery at Fawley fell considerably during the 1980s and by 1992 there were no more than 16 departures a week. On May 18, 1992 Class 37 No. 37072 passes under the signal gantry at Marchwood with 6B51, the 09.01 from Eastleigh to Fawley, which on this occasion comprised empty 45-ton tanks returning from Saltley and Bromford Bridge.

BLOCK OIL TRAIN SERVICES FROM STANLOW
WEEK COMMENCING MONDAY 8TH MAY 1989

Programme of trains to Eastern Region from Stanlow Refinery in May 1989. A considerable proportion of the oil traffic from Stanlow in the 1980s was railed across the Pennines, with 18 timetable workings to the Shell depots at Jarrow and Leeds as well as occasional specials to the Appleyard Fuel depot at Harrogate, Appleton Associates at Scarborough and the Wayahead Fuels depot at York.

remain open until 1999 the closure of many small oil depots in the south east of England, coupled with more road deliveries, meant that it loaded its last train in 1993.

In contrast, until the early 1990s Shell's biggest and busiest refinery at Stanlow, near Ellesmere Port, had continued to load up to 30 trains a week, but the closure of the large regional distribution depot at Leeds in 1995, together with the earlier closures of those at Aberystwyth, Doe Hill, Dumfries, Harrogate, Newbury, Royston, Scarborough, Swindon, Torksey, Ulverston and York, meant the loss of a significant proportion of its rail business. By 1997 only a weekly service to the general distribution depot at Whittington, near Oswestry, and intermittent trains of fuel oil to Northwich and St Helens, were still running, insufficient to justify the ongoing expense of maintaining the rail-loading facility at Stanlow from where the last train departed in March 1998. It was a similar story at Esso, who in 1983 had closed its Herbrandston refinery,

Class 60 No. 60035 'Florence Nightingale' heads the daily Robeston to Westerleigh service through Newport on August 15, 1995. Robeston refinery at Milford Haven had been opened by Amoco in 1973 with Murco (a subsidiary of Murphy Oil) becoming a part-owner in 1981. When in 1990 British Rail relaxed the requirement that Class A tank wagons must be painted grey with a red solebar, Murco was one of the first oil companies to then repaint some tank wagons into its company colours. In 2014 the refinery at Robeston was shut down and converted by its new owners, Puma Energy, into a petroleum storage and distribution terminal for imported finished product, with rail service to Bedworth, Theale and Westerleigh continuing unchanged.

In addition to the crude oil traffic from Holybourne to Fawley, there were also railborne flows of crude from Gainsborough and Welton with a daily train running to the Texaco tank farm at Immingham Docks from where the crude was either sent via pipeline to the nearby Lindsey refinery or shipped to BP's Grangemouth refinery. The workings from Gainsborough ceased in 1998 but those from the BP Developments siding at Welton, Lincolnshire, continued for a few more years. On July 9, 2002 Class 37 No. 37888 storms through Barnetby with 6D96, the 16.09 Welton to Immingham.

near Milford Haven, and transferred much of the outbound rail traffic from the refinery at Fawley to pipelines. By 1992 rail traffic at Fawley was limited to outbound flows of bitumen to Bromford Bridge and Plymouth Cattewater, LPG to Clydach and Longport, and traction gas oil to the BR locomotive depots and fuelling points at Bristol St Philip's Marsh, Cardiff Canton, Exeter, Ipswich, Margam, Penzance, Plymouth Laira, St Blazey and Saltley, while there were also inbound block trainloads of crude oil from Holybourne, Hants, along with a weekly train from the Hays chemical works at Sandbach which comprised two or three tank wagons loaded with liquid chlorine. However, all outgoing traffic ended in 2013 and when the final service from Holybourne arrived in September 2016 another major refinery had ceased to use rail. Esso's coastal terminal at Bowling and its pipeline-fed

depots at Bromford Bridge and Colwick had also loaded rail tanks, particularly with light-grade products such as motor spirit for other regional depots and traction gas oil for BR, but such tonnages were limited and this traffic fell victim to the demise of Speedlink in 1991.

Elsewhere rail traffic from Gulf's Waterston refinery at Milford Haven and Mobil's Coryton refinery at Thames Haven also gradually dwindled away during the 1990s, but the British Petroleum refinery at Grangemouth continued to supply a number of distribution depots in Scotland and the Borders. Robeston refinery at Milford Haven, which was owned by Murco, along with Conoco's Humber refinery at Immingham and Lindsey refinery at South Killingholme, the latter jointly operated by Total and Petrofina, all remained busy loading trains for the larger oil depots at Bedworth, Colnbrook, Jarrow, Kingsbury, Preston, Rectory

Junction (Nottingham), Theale and Westerleigh. In the 1990s Lindsey was also still despatching traction gas oil by rail to a handful of locomotive fuelling points but by 2015 only the weekly workings to Ipswich and Leeds Neville Hill TMD remained.

Other petroleum traffic still on rail included a twice-weekly trainload of natural gas condensate from North Walsham to the Carless refinery at Harwich and the occasional trainload of aviation spirit from Grangemouth refinery to the Rolls Royce terminal at Sinfin, near Derby, while bitumen traffic, which in the past had run from the refineries at Ardrossan, Coryton, Fawley, Llandarcy and Stanlow, was reduced to a single flow from Lindsey to Preston.

By 2018 the former refinery site at Port Clarence was no longer refining crude oil but it remained in use as a tank farm for imported refined product with a weekly service running to Cardiff Docks, while imported motor spirit was also railed from Immingham Docks to Bedworth. Imports of aviation fuel also appeared on rail in 2019, when the Lindsey to Colnbrook service was withdrawn and replaced by a working from Grain utilising a fleet of new VTG bogie tank wagons leased by BAA Logistics.

In 2018 petroleum traffic appeared to have stabilised at around four to five million tonnes a year, although with some of the remaining rail-served depots due for closure over the next few years this figure seems set to decline even further.

Fuel oil traffic had declined considerably by the 1980s but a handful of block workings survived, supplying chemical works and paper mills with regular trains running from the Shell refinery at Stanlow to the ICI works at Burn Naze, Northwich and Runcorn. Another working was the 'Fridays Only' train that ran most weeks from Lindsey Refinery to the Reed Paper Mills at Darwen, near Blackburn, that area of east Lancashire then being home to much of the country's wallpaper production. Normally the train would load to eight bogie Petrofina Class B tanks but discharge problems meant that three tanks had been left behind at Darwen when 6E67, the 13.55 FO return working to Lindsey, was recorded passing through Manchester Victoria behind a Class 47 on August 31, 1984.

The 1993 requirement to install vapour recovery systems at receiving terminals contributed to the closure of many smaller oil depots, but even some that were upgraded have faced closure in recent years as distribution networks have undergone further change and rationalisation. Class 70 No. 70816 was in charge of only its second revenue service 6E82, the 12.16 Rectory Junction to Lindsey, when photographed at Lincoln on May 23, 2017 while within two years the terminal at Rectory Junction had been listed for closure.

Until recent years traction gas oil was railed to almost all locomotive depots and fuelling points, with the refineries at Fawley, Grangemouth, Lindsey, Shellhaven and Stanlow all forwarding such traffic. However, during the 1990s most of the remaining flows were transferred to road so that by 2015 only the weekly workings to Ipswich and Leeds Neville Hill TMD remained. The Ipswich train was one of the last petroleum services to use two-axle tanks with five VTG, ex-British Petroleum TTAs seen heading through Barnetby on their way back to Lindsey in August of that year.

Unlike most other petroleum products bitumen could not be sent by pipeline, due to its high viscosity, and until the late-1980s there were regular workings from Stanlow to the bitumen terminals at Bardon Hill, Cranmore, Exeter, Filton, Hereford, Norwich, Skipton and West Drayton. Class 37 No. 37148 shunts the Anglo-American Asphalt sidings at Cranmore after arriving with 6V33, the 02.38 from Stanlow, on June 16, 1982.

The Totalfina Bitumen works at Preston Docks uses the incoming bitumen to produce asphalt paving mixtures and blocks, oxidised bitumen and bitumen emulsions, with rail access to the unloading siding being via the privately operated line from Strand Road. Until 1995 operations on the line were handled by the Borough of Preston's fleet of three 4wDH Sentinel locomotives and when responsibility for working the revived service was awarded to Ribble Rail it also acquired two of the Sentinels. Works No. RR10283 built 1968, named 'Progress', hauls a rake of empty tanks through the docks estate on its way to the exchange sidings on August 1, 2018.

Shell owned more than 400 two-axle bitumen tanks, all fitted with flame tubes in the end and 'chimneys' on top of the barrel so that the load could be reheated upon arrival to make it flow freely when being unloaded. TTA No. SUKO61340 is pictured at Prismo Universal's Bardon Hill bitumen terminal in July 1987. At Stanlow the bitumen production plant was connected to the Manchester Ship Canal Railway's line alongside Oil Sites Road, but in 1990 Shell opened a new blown bitumen unit and road tanker filling station nearby at Eastham and the rail traffic ceased.

Other bitumen workings, such as those from Llandarcy and Coryton, would eventually switch to road but bitumen continued to be railed from Lindsey refinery to the Kelbit terminal at Ashton-in-Makerfield, near Wigan, and to the Lanfina works at Preston Docks. Until 1992 the Preston Docks trains also conveyed other petroleum products, including motor spirit and kerosene, to the Petrofina depot at Preston. On April 23, 1986 a pair of Class 31s pass the closed Manchester Exchange station at the head of 7E60, the 10.40 return working from Preston, formed of 10 two-axle bitumen and about a dozen bogie and two-axle Class A tanks.

From 2004 the Preston Docks train was operated by EWS but in 2015 haulage switched to Colas resulting in the appearance of Class 56s, 60s and 70s on the working. Class 60 No. 60047 leaves the exchange sidings at Strand Road, Preston, with the 6E32 08.55 empty working for Lindsey on June 6, 2016.

In the 1980s the pool of bitumen tanks used to supply the Lanfina works at Preston included four 51-tonne glw TUA belonging to Lancashire Tar Distillers and a number of 46-tonne glw tanks on hire from Procor, with TUA No. LTD74500 and TTA No. PR58945 being recorded passing through Manchester in April 1995.

Several of the bogie tanks in use on the Lindsey to Preston working had been built by the Standard Wagon Company in 1969 for Petrofina as Class B tanks, being converted into Class A vehicles and renumbered at Railcar Services in 1981. TEA No. FINA85514 (originally FINA85602) is seen at Preston in August 1991.

The bitumen working to Preston was suspended in 1995 when the road/rail bridge that carried the line across the entrance to the docks sustained damage and when the train was eventually reinstated in 2005 a rake of 102-tonne Class B tanks on hire from British Petroleum was used. However, in December 2010 they were replaced by a new purpose-built batch of 30 ICA bogie tanks leased from VTG. The new tanks were fitted with increased insulation, to keep the bitumen between 160°C and 180°C, while a new design of heating coil made cleaning the interior simpler and safer. A new valve system meant there was no need for workers to access the top of the barrel to open the manlids while the wagons, running on TF25 'Track Friendly' bogies, could carry a 74-tonne payload. ICA No. 35 70 7790 029-2 is pictured at Preston on July 22, 2018.

Class 85 No. 85034 heads 6S99, the 18.05 TThO Runcorn Folly Lane Sidings to Stevenston, north along the WCML at Winwick Junction on August 12, 1980. At the time this was one of 18 trainloads of caustic soda timetabled to leave the ICI works at Runcorn each week, with the others running to Corkickle, Grimsby, Holywell Junction, Northwich and Seal Sands. Caustic soda, produced by the electrolysis of brine, had a wide range of applications and at ICI's Stevenston plant in North Ayrshire it was used in the manufacture of cellulose derivatives such as sodium carboxlymethyl cellulose that could be found in detergents, paints and paper products. 6S99 was withdrawn in 1985 and the caustic soda required at Stevenston, which by then had declined to about 270 tonnes a week, was then despatched from Runcorn via the Speedlink network with the programme calling for four tank wagons to be delivered every Wednesday and Friday.

Even more dramatic has been the disappearance of chemical traffic on rail, since for most of the Twentieth Century Britain was a major chemical producer with rail playing a leading role in transporting various base chemicals, compounds and intermediates between works. Given their specialist nature most chemicals were conveyed in block trains, but from the early-1980s the industry began a gradual switch away from inorganic towards the organic and fine chemicals sector which involved fewer rail movements. Consequently overall chemical tonnages on rail fell by around a half with much of what remained transferred to the wagonload network.

Speedlink's closure in July 1991 resulted in more traffic being lost although an attempt was made to retain some of this high value tonnage by the introduction of a number of 'Contract Services'. Most 'Contract Services' were timetabled to run directly between private sidings, although a few were scheduled to follow a more complicated route in order to serve several customers and handle a mix of different traffics. Unfortunately within a few years many had proved to be uneconomic and

were withdrawn. A bright spot in BR's chemical portfolio was the various cross-Channel flows routed via the Dover to Dunkirk train ferry which had survived the end of Speedlink courtesy of Railfreight Distribution's new 'Connectrail' services. These mixed freights, running from Dover to Bescot, Cardiff, Crewe and Willesden, were introduced to retain as much international traffic as possible in the run up to the opening of the Channel Tunnel. Indeed changes within the global chemical industry brought additional tonnage to some cross-Channel chemical flows, one unexpected development in the early 1990s resulting in an increase in the amount of anti-knock compound railed from Britain to the continent at a time when the switch towards unleaded fuel was already underway. It was a short-term gain, caused by the closure of an anti-knock plant in Germany and the rundown of similar facilities in France and Italy, but a gain nonetheless.

However, the final sailing of the Dover to Dunkirk train ferry on December 22, 1995 brought an end to such Anglo-continental workings given that almost all dangerous

goods were barred from the Channel Tunnel. A handful of domestic chemical flows, such as caustic soda and nitric acid to Sellafield and hydrochloric acid to Dalry, would remain on rail for a few more years, while the movement of arcton from Runcorn to the continent returned to rail in 2003. However, that traffic ended in 2009 and whereas in 1980 there had still been more than 2000 chemical tank wagons in regular service on Britain's rail network, 30 years later there was almost none.

ICI's fleet of two-axle vacuum-braked anhydrous ammonia tanks were replaced in 1985 by a pool of air-braked bogie gas tanks leased from STS and VTG, but cheap imported fertiliser would bring an end to the anhydrous ammonia workings. TIA No. 33 70 7892 002-8 is seen at Tees Yard in March 1991 soon after the traffic had finished.

Fisons Fertilisers ammonium nitrate traffic suffered an even earlier demise. When new in 1959 the fleet of 45 vacuum-braked 35-ton glw tanks had been based at their Stanford-le-Hope works, but by the early 1980s they were to be found working from the Fisons plant at Avonmouth to the company's fertiliser works at Cliff Quay, Ipswich, and at Widnes. TSV No. FF47395 was photographed at Bristol in August 1980 four years before the traffic ceased.

The large ICI complex at Billingham produced a wide range of ammonia-based chemicals, and trainloads of anhydrous ammonia, for use in the manufacture of compound fertilisers, regularly despatched to other ICI works at Heysham, Leith and Severn Beach. Class 31 No. 31134 drifts through Skipton with 6E91, the 11.26 Heysham to Haverton Hill, formed of discharged 40-ton glw anhydrous ammonia tanks, on November 12, 1981. Note the inclusion of a former BR ferry van as a barrier vehicle between the locomotive and the tank wagons, while out of sight at the rear of the train would have been another barrier vehicle and a Brake Van. In 1985 these two-axle vacuum-braked anhydrous ammonia tanks were replaced on the Heysham service by air-braked bogie tanks, but the working would only continue until April 1986 with the fertiliser works at Heysham closing the following year.

Although caustic soda traffic from ICI's Castner-Kellner Works in Runcorn declined considerably in the mid-1980s, some of the slack was taken up by new wagonload flows from Eastham, near Ellesmere Port, where the Pan Ocean tank farm began loading caustic soda destined for British Cellophane at Bridgwater and the Glaxo antibiotics plant at Ulverston. Running via Speedlink these workings utilised wagons previously hired by ICI and, with its ICI roundel only recently and rather crudely painted over, No. TRL 70701 is pictured at the end of the Eastham branch on March 21, 1987. As a 51-tonne glw tank its TOPS code should have been TUA but finding a TTA code painted in the data panel was a not uncommon occurrence with such wagons.

Some low volume chemical traffics had always relied upon the wagonload network as did the movement of chemical tank wagons to and from repair. Two Procor 45-tonne sodium hypochlorite tanks, Nos. PR58213 and PR58216, were returning to ICI's Castner-Kellner Works at Runcorn after repair at Horbury Junction wagon works when photographed in the consist of a Healey Mills to Warrington service at Warrington Bank Quay in August 1984. ICI leased six of these tank wagons for its 'Hypo' traffic from Runcorn which ran to Willesden as part of a mixed chemical service that also conveyed caustic soda and solvents such as methyl chloroform and trichloroethylene. However, the despatch of sodium hypochlorite (the active component of household bleach) by rail from Runcorn would end in 1986.

Some CO2 traffic was retained after the end of Speedlink in July 1991 when new 'Contract Services' began running from Billingham and Cameron Bridge to Coleshill and Willesden, while four 'Contract Services' were also introduced to handle traffic from the BP Chemicals plant at Hull Saltend. They included direct trains from Hull to Baglan Bay and Seal Sands (both of which carried acetic acid) and to Spondon conveying both acetic acid and acetone. The fourth working was a thrice-weekly service which ran to Ellesmere Port before then continuing on to Mostyn Dock, on the north Wales coast. This train included tanks of acetic anhydride, which was used by Warwick Chemicals at Mostyn Dock in the production of low-temperature detergent additives, as well as tanks of acetone eventually destined for Glaxo Pharmaceuticals at Ulverston or Roche Products at Dalry, which would be detached when the train called at Ellesmere Port. This stop was also an opportunity to pick up tanks of imported acetic acid destined for the Courtaulds Acetates plant at Spondon which had been loaded at the GATX tank farm at Eastham, these reaching their final destination via Mostyn Dock and Hull. Class 37 no. 37242 had 15 TTAs in tow, 10 from Mostyn, three from Ulverston, and two from Dalry, as it headed east through Eccles station on September 9, 1991 with 6E39, the 09.15 MWFO Mostyn Dock to Hull.

LEFT: Carbon dioxide was also handled at Ardwick West freight depot with regular deliveries arriving from the ICI plant at Billingham. Four discharged CO2 tanks bring up the rear of Trip No. 33 seen slipping through Ashburys station on its way from Ardwick to Ashburys East Yard in August 1985.

Not all the traffic from BP Chemicals at Hull could be kept on rail after July 1991 and among the losses was the movement of acetone to the Royal Ordnance Factory at Bishopton where it was used as a solvent in the production of explosives. BP Chemicals leased 106 STS 45-ton Class A tank wagons to carry the various chemicals produced at Hull, including No. STS 53315 recorded in the rural surroundings of the Bishopton factory site on July 25, 1990.

Most chemical traffic ran directly between major production plants but a handful of chemicals could be found being handled at local goods depots. These included the movement of various fire-retardants produced at Ciba Geigy's Trafford Park works for use in plasticisers which had been loaded into ferry tank wagons at Trafford Park. However, when the entire rail system within the Trafford Park industrial estate was mothballed in 1984 the Ciba Geigy plant lost its own connection, and so loading of the STS ferry tanks was switched to Manchester's Ardwick West FD. The fire-retardants were exported to Switzerland and TIB No. 23 70 7397 100-2 waits to be loaded at Ardwick West in July 1985 a year or so before the traffic ended.

The Associated Octel Co. was a long-standing BR customer and its works at Ellesmere Port, which opened in 1954 to produce anti-knock compound, continued to despatch rail traffic both by the trainload and by the wagonload after the end of Speedlink. The trainload movements included a daily service from Ellesmere Port to Octel's bromine extraction plant at Amlwch, on Anglesey, conveying liquid chlorine to north Wales and returning with ethylene dibromide for use in the process at Ellesmere Port, while there was also a thrice-weekly block train of chlorine which ran to the Albright and Wilson works at Langley Green. With four loaded chlorine tanks and two discharged ethylene dibromide tanks from the Associated Octel works in tow, Manchester Ship Canal Co. 0-6-0DH Sentinel No. 3003 heads for the BR sidings at Ellesmere Port East on October 26, 1990.

BELOW: Cross-Channel chemical traffic remained buoyant until 1995 and on April 25 Class 08 No. 08913 shunts VTG bogie tank No. 3380 7794 002-5 in Dover Town Yard. The tank, which was loaded with methyl chloride, was en route from Stade, near Hamburg, to Dow Corning at Barry where the chemical was used in the production of silicon compounds.

In 1984 the wagon lessors STS (Storage and Transport Systems) had also launched a spot hire arrangement for chemical customers marketed under the brand name 'RailCALL' whereby they could hire a vehicle for one specific transit. Customers to avail themselves of this service included Hickson and Welch of Castleford and Laporte Chemicals in Warrington, but after initial interest the scheme gradually faded away. A line of four TIA 46-tonne stainless steel ferry tanks including No. 23 70 7390 028-2, previously used to carry the dyestuffs intermediates orthochloroaniline and orthotoluidene from Castleford to Germany, are pictured in store at Warrington Dallam freight depot awaiting their next spot hire in June 1985.

Concerns over the storage of large quantities of chlorine saw both the Amlwch and Langley Green trains withdrawn at the end of 1993, but Octel's cross-Channel wagonload traffic via the train ferry continued until the summer of 1995 and on April 5, 1994 MSC No. 3003 was spotted bringing seven ferry tank wagons out of the Octel works at Ellesmere Port. Immediately behind the Sentinel are four anti-knock tanks, two of which were destined for the Exxon oil refinery at Novara in north west Italy, while the third was en route to the Szazhalombatta refinery in Hungary and the fourth to the Societe Octel Kuhlmann works situated on the Loire at Paimbœuf, France. The fifth and seventh wagons were discharged bogie ethyl chloride tanks on their way back to Huls Chemicals at Marl in the German state of North Rhine-Westphalia, while the sixth wagon was a loaded bogie sodium tank also heading for Paimbœuf.

In 1994 Associated Octel was still operating more than 60 anti-knock ferry tanks from its plant at Ellesmere Port, although given their highly dangerous cargo they were subjected to frequent and extensive maintenance and so would make relatively few loaded journeys a year. An unusually dirty TIA No. 23 70 7490 413-6 leaves Ellesmere Port in August 1991 bound for the OMV oil refinery at Schwechat, near Vienna.

Although the movement of anti-knock compound in tank wagons ended in 1995 some export traffic would continue to be conveyed by rail, loaded into Octel drums and tank containers. On July 9, 1999 Class 66 No. 66099 heads a Ditton to Immingham Docks working through the rebuilt Manchester Victoria with two drums of anti-knock, strapped to a bulkhead flat, on the leading Megafret container flat.

Arcton (chlorodifluoromethane), used in refrigeration and air conditioning systems, had last been forwarded by rail in the 1980s so its return in 2003 came as something of a surprise. Again this development was driven by the closure of production capacity on the continent but in the intervening years Rocksavage Works in Runcorn had lost its internal rail connection and so, first the AHC Warehousing siding at Ditton and then Warrington Dallam freight depot were used as the loading points, the arcton being brought by road from Runcorn. Two bogie VTG tanks were being loaded at Dallam in June 2008.

CHAPTER 15

The vast majority of tank wagons have always been privately owned given their specialist loads and until the 1960s many that remained in service were still unfitted and with payloads of under 20 tons. Even when BR had begun to modernise its own freight stock some tank owners were slow to do likewise, including the Burmah Oil Trading Co. who had inherited a rather motley collection of elderly tank wagons with their acquisition of Castrol, Lobitos and Manchester Oil Refineries Ltd. Many of the tanks acquired by Burmah were well over 30 years old, and while their main line use was limited, those based at the Manchester Oil Refineries works in Trafford Park continued to be used to carry base lubricating oil to the Burmah Oil blending plant at Hyde Central, near Stockport, until 1973. The oldest wagon in the Manchester Oil Refineries fleet was No. 1, a typical 12-ton capacity cradle-mounted design built in 1923, which would even survive in traffic long enough to be allocated the TOPS number BOTM40074 (BOTM – Burmah Oil Trading Manchester). Having been withdrawn in 1973 No. 1 went from Trafford Park to the Wagon Repairs Ltd. works at Mold Junction where, rather than being cut up, it was retained in internal use for several years. After closure of the Mold Junction works the tank then moved to the Wagon Repairs works at Gloucester before arriving at Railcar Services, Stoke, where it was recorded still in MOR livery on March 23, 1991.

A Tank Wagon Selection

LEFT: Esso was the first of the major oil companies to begin updating its wagon fleet when in 1957 it purchased more than 1000 23.5-ton capacity, 35 ton glw, tanks that were 23ft 8½in over headstocks with a 15ft wheelbase. The barrel was attached to the underframe by four support brackets, while the wagons were vacuum-braked and fitted with roller bearing axleboxes so that they could run at 60mph. Between 1957 and 1962 some 1315 would be built for Esso, including wagons suitable for bitumen as well as for Class A and Class B products, and they helped pave the way for the dramatic rise in petroleum traffic working in block trains from Fawley to various Esso distribution depots including Bromford Bridge, Northampton, Reading and Tiverton. When no longer required by Esso some were sold to the Central Electricity Generating Board and TSV No. CEGB48541 (formerly ESSO43879) was recorded at Drakelow Power Station in February 1988.

In 1964 an axleload of 22½ tons was approved by BR, and Esso ordered a number of 45-ton glw 'monobloc' tanks, although in this instance they would be leased from BRTE (British Railway Traffic & Electric Co.) rather than purchased outright. With a tare weight of 14 tons Class B tanks were able to carry a payload of approximately 31 tons, while Class A tanks could accommodate 28 tons of motor spirit. In later years many of the BRTE tanks found their way into the service of other oil companies, vacuum-braked TTF No. BRT57044 having last been on hire to Charrington Gardner & Locket when recorded at Horbury Junction awaiting disposal in February 1987.

With the increase in axleload, attention had also turned towards bogie tank design and a 92-tonne glw prototype was soon developed for SM&BP by wagon builder Metro-Cammell. Given the intrinsic strength of the tank barrel continuous solebars were dispensed with, the barrel being secured only to two short sections situated over each English Steel bogie. The solebars then angled down and inwards to join two steel members running along the underside of the tank to which were fitted the brake gear and discharge pipes. End ladders and full-length catwalks gave access to the filling hatches and once uprated to 102-tonne glw, which was approved on specified major routes, SM&BP would eventually order more than 1000 of these bogie vehicles. Still sporting the early Shell logo, TEA No. SUKO87103 was recorded at Manchester Victoria when en route from Stanlow to Leeds in September 1987.

RIGHT: A number of variations in the 102t glw design would later appear including full-length solebars, modified ladders and catwalks, Gloucester, Y25, or Schlieren bogies, with every oil major either owning or leasing its own bogie tanks. However, by the new millennium wagon lessor CAIB was looking to replace its now life-expired fleet and during 2001 some 114 new bogie tank wagons were built by Marcroft Engineering of Stoke, the first 93 being fitted with Powell Duffryn Rail TF25 low track-force bogies with bogie-mounted brake cylinders and handwheels. Sixty of these tanks were allocated to petroleum traffic from Humberside including TEA No. CAIB88077 seen at Kingsbury in September 2002.

The acceptance of a 25-ton axleload on approved routes also encouraged a few companies to purchase 50-ton glw tank wagons fitted with either English Steel or Gloucester pedestal suspension. However, with the oil companies and wagon lessors having already invested heavily in the more versatile 45-tonners, the 50-ton tanks were not built in large numbers. TUB No. TRL70900, a lagged Class B tank built originally for Petrofina, had been sold to Tiger Rail Leasing when recorded at Procor's Horbury Junction wagon works in May 1988.

The other 21 tanks built at Stoke during 2001 differed in having straight-frame TF25 bogies and body-mounted brakes. They were also completed as CAIB was sold to VTG and hence were delivered with a VTG number prefix. Initially leased by Petroplus to carry dev and kerosene from Port Clarence to Bedworth and Westerleigh, TEA No. VTG88108 was recorded in the repair sidings at Port Clarence in August 2004.

Shell Mex & BP had been slower to update their wagon fleet but in 1964 they placed orders for some 2,700 45-ton glw 'monobloc' tank wagons. Furthermore, those built from January 1966 would be air-braked, and at the same time large numbers of air-braked 45-ton tanks were built for many of the other oil companies. TOPS coded TTA No. SUKO60513 is pictured at Ellesmere Port East Sidings, near Stanlow, in December 1986. This Class A tank had been Epikote lined so that it was suitable for carrying aviation fuel.

By the 1940s tank wagon design had moved on with the barrel now usually being attached to the underframe by centrally situated anchor mounts, while capacities had increased with 20-ton becoming the new norm. Like the saddle-mounted tanks most of the early unfitted anchor-mounted wagons had been withdrawn by the mid-1970s, but one large fleet to survive in service was that belonging to the National Coal Board for the carriage of crude coal tar. More than 100 would remain in traffic until 1982, working from several coke works in South Wales and the north east of England to the Thomas Ness tar distillation works at Caerphilly. Their final use was in carrying imported tar from Cardiff Dock to Caerphilly, No. NCB48364, TOPS code TSO, being recorded at Cardiff Docks in October 1981.

The increase in permitted axleloads also encouraged the development of the 'monobloc' tank design where the chassis cross-members dipped below the level of the solebar. This enabled a larger diameter barrel to be fitted while still remaining within the loading gauge, the barrel being bolted to wing plates that were welded along the top of the solebar. The larger barrel allowed more of the lighter and less dense petroleum fractions, such as naphtha and motor spirit, to be carried and 350 Class A 35-ton glw 'monobloc' tanks were built in 1963 for Esso by Charles Roberts and Powell Duffryn. By the late 1980s few remained in service but TSV No. ESSO45062, pictured at Winnington Power Station in February 1988, was one of 20 tanks used to carry waste oil between Winnington and Drakelow.

CHAPTER 16

Departmental Developments

During the 1970s railway ballast was still sourced from several quarries situated around the country. On July 22, 1983 Class 25 No. 25145 prepares to couple up to a rake of Catfish and Dogfish ballast hoppers at ARC's Ribblehead Quarry sidings which will then form 7E54, the 10.22 to Healey Mills Engineers Sidings. *(©Trevor Mann collection)*

Until the late 1980s railway ballast was obtained from a number of quarries with each supplying their local region. The Southern Region obtained much of its ballast from Meldon Quarry, near Okehampton, while the northern half of the London Midland Region was served by Bayston Hill Quarry, situated near Shrewsbury, Blodwell Quarry on the former Cambrian Railway branch line from Oswestry, and quarries near Ribblehead on the Settle & Carlisle line.

New ballast would be loaded during the week, most commonly into trains of purpose-built BR two-axle and bogie hopper wagons, which were then despatched to Civil Engineers yards from where they would be ready to emerge for use during weekend engineering possessions. At the same time trains of open wagons, some built for the departmental fleet and others ex-revenue vehicles eking out their final years, would be deployed to remove spent ballast and other railway spoil for disposal at one of the many BR-owned tips situated around the network.

However, firstly railfreight sectorisation and then the restructuring of the industry in the lead up to privatisation, brought these operations into sharper focus. Until 1994 regional Civil Engineers had relied upon traction being freely available when required, but now Railtrack, as the new infrastructure owner, had to buy in train services from the operating companies and a rationalisation of departmental workings soon took place. Firstly the number of quarries supplying new railway ballast was reduced to just four, while many engineers' yards and sidings were closed as the formation of possession trains was concentrated on 16 local distribution centres. Many of these LDCs would also be the location of a 'virtual quarry', where not only was new ballast stockpiled but waste ballast graded and, when suitable, the stone recycled either for further use by the railway or sold to the construction industry.

At the same time the wagon fleet was gradually upgraded as the last of the vacuum-braked ballast and spoil wagons were replaced by newer larger air-braked vehicles. Many of these 'new' wagons were rebuilds of former BR revenue stock, but as the 1990s progressed large purpose-built bogie wagons were added to the departmental fleet. A fleet of new 77-tonne capacity box wagons enabled the running of 2000-tonne trains between quarry and virtual quarry, resulting in better use of traction and train crew resources, while the ballast hopper fleet was supplemented by the 62-tonne Autoballasters, some rebuilt from relatively new Tiphook aggregate hoppers and others purchased new by Railtrack and then Network Rail.

Both Network Rail and EWS also made a considerable investment in upgrading departmental wagon types and in purchasing new rolling stock and on-track plant and equipment.

From being the poor relation, reliant on hand-me-downs and cast-offs, on today's railway infrastructure workings have become some of the most modern and varied of all railway operations.

Class 40 No. 40009 heads through the closed Manchester Exchange station in August 1983 with a short St Helens Shaw Street to Guide Bridge ballast train. Formed of just three loaded bogie Sealion ballast hoppers, this was an additional working, the engineers yard at Guide Bridge being the destination for a daily timetabled ballast train from Bayston Hill Quarry, near Shrewsbury.

In addition to spent ballast all manner of waste materials including demolition debris would be railed to the spoil tips and ZGV No. DS 13228 was carrying such a load when spotted at Southend Central in July 1979. Besides the wagons' Es branding and 'D' number prefix the green painted triangle was a further indication of its allocation to the Civil Engineers. Also just in shot, and similarly loaded, can be seen ZGV No. DB 495812, an all steel bodied Highfit which was another type commonly found in engineers traffic by the 1970s

The Mermaids were useful when reballasting double track as their entire contents could be deposited in the adjacent formation, as illustrated by this view of Class 40 No. 40143 with a ballast train at Frodsham station in the early 1980s. *(© Dave Millward)*

The 40t Sealion dual-braked bogie ballast hoppers, of which 460 were built by BR between 1971 and 1974, could trace their origins back to the 1920s when the London & South Western Railway had begun building bogie hopper wagons for the transport of ballast from its quarry at Meldon. BR had continued to build similar vehicles, initially vacuum-braked, from 1954 and the dual-braked Sealion would remain in service into the new millennium. YGH No. DB 982579 had even been repainted in Loadhaul livery when photographed at Crewe Gresty Lane in July 2000.

BR's large fleet of purpose-built two-axle ballast hoppers included the 17t Mackarel, the 19t Catfish and the 24t Dogfish which, unlike the two smaller designs, could discharge some of its load to the side rather than just between the rails. Some 1249 Dogfish were built between 1956 and 1961 and many remained in service into the 1990s. ZFV DB 992950, built in 1956, had lasted long enough to be painted in the Civil Engineers 'Dutch' livery, but along with several others it was spotted awaiting cutting up at Barry in August 1991.

BR also built a fleet of more than 600 14t side-tipping ballast wagons that were given the Fishkind name Mermaid and coded ZJV on TOPS. They also lasted until the 1990s with ZJV No. DB 989298 being recorded at Chester Wagon Shops in May 1994.

Mixed wagon formations were also quite common for ballast trains and Class 47 No. 47333 had two Sealion, five Catfish and two Dogfish in tow as it headed a Guide Bridge to Wigan working past Manchester Victoria East signal-box in October 1991.

Until the mid-1990s there were more than 20 rail-served spoil tips situated across the country for the disposal of spent ballast, old sleepers and miscellaneous waste material such as demolition rubble, and after weekend engineering works trainloads of spoil would run to the nearest tip. Motive power for the humble spoil trip was usually a Type 2 or Type 3 diesel and Class 25 No. 25036 heads a Crewe to Ince Moss Tip working past Winwick in August 1980. The train is typical for the period, formed of a mix of Medfits, Grampus, Highfits and Shoc Opens.

In the early 1980s unfitted pre-nationalisation five-plank open wagons were still to be seen in spoil traffic and former Southern Railway ZGO No. DS 12409 was spotted at Ely, when en route to the tip at Chesterton Junction, on August 29, 1979.

The early 1990s saw several hundred 21t Coal hoppers modified for spoil traffic having their bodies cut down, doors sealed and new numbers for their new role. Code named Tope ZCV No. DB 970725 was at Tees Yard in June 1994.

The BR-built Medfits found little use in revenue service but were popular with the Civil Engineers as their low sides made them difficult to overload and easy to unload. Most had gone by the early 1990s but ZDV No. ADB 461051, previously allocated to the Electrification Concreting Unit, was still in general rubbish/spoil traffic when recorded at Crewe Gresty Road in March 1996.

LEFT: Class 37 No. 37025 waits for its train of Dogfish to be loaded with locally quarried ballast at the Kyle of Lochalsh in July 1983.

Class 31 No. 31146 passes the platforms of the closed Manchester Exchange station with 9H25, the 13.05 SX CCE trip from Ince Moss Tip to Guide Bridge Brookside Sidings, on September 4, 1986. The train consists of empty 16t Minerals that had been reassigned to spoil traffic.

In 1984 a large number of 16-tonne Mineral wagons were recoded ZHV and transferred to the Civil Engineers, but as spoil is a denser load than coal, problems were encountered in overloading them. Consequently the ZHVs had two large slots cut in their sides to obviate this danger, but they were withdrawn after a few years. ZHV No. DB 550412 is seen at Birkenhead Docks in April 1985.

Although built to carry new sleepers (note the cast plate which reads 'Return Empty To Ditton Sleeper Depot') by 1980 the LMS-built three-plank Haddock were in spoil traffic. ZCO No. DM 749442 (which has received a 'DB' number prefix in error) is seen at Watford Junction in August 1980. Like the five-plank opens these wagons had been withdrawn from service by the middle of the decade.

Not all the wagons found in spoil traffic were ex-revenue vehicles, for between 1951 and 1961 BR had built some 4781 three-door 20-tonne Grampus which were suitable for carrying ballast, spoil and general materials. Of these some 3840 were unfitted but vacuum-braked Grampus ZBV No. DB 991798, built in 1959, is pictured at Swansea Burrows Sidings in October 1994. Its rusty black livery was typical for these wagons.

A development of the Dolphin, the 50t low-floor rail wagons were named Sturgeon. From 1978 some Sturgeon were fitted with air-brakes at which point they were renamed as Tench, with one providing the sole load for Class 31 No. 31416 as it heads 6F67, the 09.02 Guide Bridge to Wigan through Manchester Victoria in May 1989.

For the carriage of 60ft lengths of rail the LNER developed a 40t capacity low-floor bogie wagon fitted with 2ft 6in diameter wheels and the design would eventually be developed into a 50t vehicle. Being fitted with either hinged or removable sides they were useful for carrying a variety of other loads such as rail chairs, scrap lengths of rail and sleepers. Given the Fishkind name Dolphin, YAO No. DE 544345, built at Dukinfield in 1939 and initially allocated to Guide Bridge, is seen at Northampton Bridge Street Pre-Assembly Depot in October 1979.

EWS continued with the Sea Urchin rebuilding programme and ZCA No. DC 200357, rebuilt from a VCA, was seen at Crewe Gresty Lane engineers yard on August 2, 1998.

The small yard at Oxford Hinksey had recently been brought back into use as a mini 'virtual quarry' and stabling point for engineers traffic in this May 2005 view.

After they were no longer required for revenue service a number of air-braked open wagons were used to carry sleepers, as seen in this view of Class 08 No. 08676 shunting the small engineers yard at Oxford Hinksey in May 2005.

In 1991 BR embarked on a rebuilding programme, fitting new low-sided box bodies to underframes recovered from some of the air-braked opens and vans made redundant by the closure of the Speedlink network. Named Sea Urchins they were then used by the Civil Engineers for general materials. Some of the rebuilding work was contracted to Marcroft Engineering and ZCA No. DC 210292, formerly a VDA, is pictured at its Stoke Wagon Works in March 1993.

The decline in coal traffic saw many MGR HAAs become redundant and more than 600 would eventually be converted into general purpose engineers wagons by the fitting of a low-sided body. Recoded MHA No. 394263 was among the first to be converted and is seen at Stoke Cockshute Yard in August 1998 during the time when this location was in use as a grading point for recovered ballast.

Former revenue stock was also used to carry sleepers and in the 1980s a large pool of 22.5t Tube wagons was reallocated to this traffic, including STV No. B 730519 seen awaiting repair at Ashton Road C&W, Manchester, in April 1986. This was one of 32 Tubes that in the 1960s had been fitted with an additional side plank and extended ends in order to carry double-stacked casks of ale from the Bass and Worthington breweries at Burton-on-Trent.

As well as the Tubes a large number of vacuum-braked Pipe wagons were transferred to the departmental fleet during the 1980s as general material carriers. Subsequently some were fitted with a through air pipe, including ZDW No. B741251 photographed at Ditton sleeper creosoting depot in August 1998. The wagon's pale blue livery indicates it had previously been allocated to 'Project Mercury', a scheme that involved the laying of a new telecommunications network along some of the main trunk routes.

When the CAIB JNAs built for Railtrack went off hire in 2009 they were replaced by a fleet of 120 IOA bogie high side opens built for Network Rail by Greenbrier Europe. Like the JNAs they are used to deliver new ballast to the stockpiles at 'virtual quarries' and LDCs (local distribution centres). Class 66 No. 66428 heads down the WCML near Crewe Basford Hall on May 21, 2019 with 20 IOAs forming 6U77, the 13.42 from Mountsorrel to Crewe Basford Hall.

While the Railtrack custodianship of Britain's rail network will not be remembered with any great fondness, it did mark the beginning of a period of major investment in new departmental rolling stock. These included a fleet of 120 JNA bogie box wagons built by Marcroft Engineering in 1998 and leased from CAIB, which were used in block trains to deliver new ballast. JNA No. CAIB3418 is pictured at Guide Bridge 'virtual quarry' in September 1998.

Other modern ballast carriers include the fleet of 355 Autoballasters, 105 of which were converted from former 62-tonne capacity Tiphook bogie aggregate hoppers by equipping them with four new electrically controlled discharge doors beneath the hopper body. JJA No. NR12949 (previously 83 70 6905 007-3 and converted by Wabtec at Doncaster in 2001) is pictured at Crewe in May 2018. This was one of the Tiphook hoppers with a cut-down body from its days working for Buxton Lime Industries between Tunstead and Hindlow.

Given the Fishkind name Mussel the IOAs can carry 77 tonnes and are used solely for the delivery of new ballast from designated quarries to local distribution centres, being prohibited from use in possession work. IOA No. 31 70 5992 055-1 is seen at Crewe in May 2019.

The first 300 MRAs were delivered in Railtrack's grey and blue livery but when a further 100, to a modified design, were acquired in 2004 they arrived in Network Rail yellow. One of the generator-equipped MRAs No. 501307 heads north at Hellifield in June 2018.

BELOW: In 2001 a fleet of new 56-tonne capacity bogie side-tipping ballast wagons took to the rails. TOPS-coded MRA they are fitted with a two-part box body, each part capable of being tipped independently, and are marshalled in sets of five with one of the end wagons in each set being fitted with a centrally located generator unit. However, in recent years some of these generators have been removed or disabled with the wagons being unloaded by grab. Class 66 No. 66426 heads through Hellifield with the 09.39 Mountsorrel to Carlisle, formed of 25 MRAs on June 5, 2018.

Redundant OBA and SPA wagons transferred to the departmental fleet were recoded ZDA and ZAA respectively with both types being used to carry miscellaneous materials including concrete troughing and steel channel. ZAA No. DC 460124 was spotted passing through Manchester Victoria when en route from Newton Heath Concrete Works to Carnforth in October 1987.

Like British Rail both Network Rail and EWS also found the need for a fleet of general-purpose low-sided box wagons that could be used to carry either ballast, spoil, or miscellaneous material such as scrap rail. However, these wagons would be air-braked bogie vehicles built new for departmental service with payloads in excess of 60 tonnes, the first to arrive in 2003 being the 555 JNAs built by Trinity at its Astra-Vagoane facility in Romania. JNA No. NLU29245 is pictured at Crewe Gresty Lane engineers' yard in January 2005.

Since 2006 more newly built general-purpose air-braked bogie low-sided box wagons have been added to the Network Rail fleet, including 40 IEAs and 140 MLAs. All are capable of carrying 66 tonnes and MLA No. 503112 was loaded with spent ballast when recorded passing Crewe Basford Hall Junction in April 2019.

Irrespective of ownership all these new infrastructure wagons were leased to Network Rail and so could be found working together irrespective of whichever freight operating company was hauling the service. On April 8, 2019 Class 66s Nos. 66305 and 66597 head south at Hellifield with the 12.46 Carlisle to Crewe Basford Hall engineers train consisting of an IEA, an MLA and eight JNA.

In 2016 some 210 Bogie Bolster D and Boplate wagons were rebuilt with box bodies by Axiom Rail at Stoke for DB Schenker and recoded as MXAs for departmental traffic. With a load of sand MXA No. 951061 arrives at Crewe Basford Hall from Toton in April 2019.

Until the widespread adoption of continuously welded rail, 60ft track panels were normally fabricated at the regional PADs (pre-assembly depots) such as those at Ashford, Crewe, Fazakerley and Taunton. The panels were then delivered on 62ft-long Salmon bogie rail wagons, a type first developed by the LMS which differed from the LNER-designed Dolphin and Sturgeon in being without sides or ends. YMO No. DB 996169 is pictured at St Helens Shaw Street Engineers Sidings in April 1984.

From the late 1990s rails and sleepers were delivered separately to engineering possessions and many of the surviving Salmon, which had been recoded YWA after the fitting of air-brakes and ASF 'Ride Control' bogies, were then used as sleeper carriers. YWA No. DB 996361 is seen at Crewe Basford Hall Junction when en route to North Wembley loaded with 112 concrete sleepers in July 2016.

In addition during 2009, following a number of instances where poorly secured recovered track panels became out of gauge, some 200 air-braked Salmon were fitted with large rectangular end pillars and central stanchions. Named Osprey the new pillars were wide enough to fit within the track gauge thus locking the panels in place, as seen in this view of YKA No. DB996405 recorded at Hellifield in July 2019.

BELOW: Between 1959 and 1961 Derby Works built 135 Borail EB and 30 Borail EC wagons, all of which were vacuum-braked and fitted with plateback bogies. The Borail EBs were for the carriage of new rail from steel mills to the various track pre-assembly depots around the network, while the Borail ECs, which did not have bolsters, were for the movement of pre-stressed concrete beams. However, by 1981 the concrete beam traffic had finished and that year a programme was begun to modernise 150 Borails by fitting them with air-brakes and Y25C bogies. Originally TOPS-coded BRA they were transferred to the engineers fleet in 1983 being recoded YLA and given the code name Mullet. Many could still be found in service more than 20 years later carrying 120ft lengths of rail from Workington steelworks to the long-welded rail depots at Castleton and Eastleigh. Corus (ex-British Steel) No. 404, a 1979-built Hunslet 0-6-0DH works No. HE8978, propels a pair of loaded Borails from the rail loading gantry towards Workington Down Yard in April 2005.

Until the 1980s lengths of long welded rail were carried by rakes of modified ex-Double Bolster wagons, but these were replaced in 1984 when BR purchased 16 purpose-built trains from Cowans Sheldon and Plasser & Theurer formed of YEA bogie LWR carriers. Class 66 No. 66020 arrives at Didcot with a train of YEAs from Eastleigh LWR depot in May 2015.

By 2018 all of the freight train operating companies were contracted to haul engineering services, with the 15.13 from Toton North Yard to Crewe Basford Hall then a GBRf working. Class 66 No. 66745 is seen approaching Crewe on April 18, 2018, the train being formed of an MLA and five MHA loaded with sand followed by a set of Network Rail LWR wagons.

Further new rail-carrying wagons had been introduced by Network Rail in March 2002 when 40 Tiphook KFA bogie container flats were converted into LWR wagons, while a further 70 rail carriers, built new by WH Davis and TOPS coded JZA, were added to the fleet later that same year. KFA No. NLU93270 is pictured under the loading gantry at Castleton LWR depot in July 2002, while JZA No. NLU93601 was photographed at Carlisle Kingmoor in June 2005. Like the earlier YEAs, the KFAs and JZAs can carry rails stacked in four tiers.

Each Long Welded Rail Train also includes both a power wagon and a rail handling wagon fitted with hydraulically actuated clamps to lift and feed each length of rail through chutes on to the ground. Rail Handling Wagon No. NLU93249 was photographed at Castleton in July 2002.

Modernising the On-Track Plant

A familiar sight on Western Region were its 10 diesel hydraulic cranes (five 10-ton and five 15-ton capacity) which were built by Booth's of Leeds in 1958/59 and allocated to Bristol, Exeter, Newport, Reading and Swansea. Two of the 15-ton Booth cranes were based at Bristol and No. DRA 81552 (previously numbered DB 352), together with its bogie match wagon No. DW 107113, is seen at Hallen Marsh Junction, Avonmouth, on resignalling work in April 1980. Like the Western's other 15-ton Booth cranes DRA 81552 had been air braked in 1978, while its cab had been modernised and refurbished with noise insulation, new lighting, an engine warning system and safe load indicators. It would remain in service until 1995 before eventually being sold to the Dean Forest Railway in 2000.

Following rail privatisation the use of New Track Construction machines for laying new sleepers and long-welded rail on to a pre-prepared track bed became almost universal. At an engineering possession new sleepers are lifted from trailing sleeper-carrying wagons by means of the NTC machine's sleeper handling gantry and placed on to the reception wagons conveyor system. This then transfers them to the head of the truss beam whereby they can be placed on to the track bed using the sleeper-drop mechanism. At the same time new lengths of rail, which have been laid ahead of the NTC machine, are thimbled through a series of rollers and clamps along the truss beam and thus aligned into the sleeper seats. The rail is then clipped to the sleepers using equipment mounted to the reception wagon as the machine slowly moves forward along the newly laid track. Grant Renewals Harsco NTC machine No. 6100930 is seen at Newport Alexandra Dock Junction in May 2005. Nearest the camera is the sleeper handling gantry, carried by KFA wagon No. CAIB 95384, with No. CAIB 95378 carrying the truss beam/sleeper-drop mechanism. In operation the truss beam is angled down off the end of the wagon to the track bed, and in optimum conditions the machine can lay sleepers at a rate of 12 per minute.

Also in the Civil Engineers fleet were a number of Light Duty Cranes which were employed on yard duties and at Pre-Assembly Depots. The Taylor & Hubbard 7½-ton Diesel Electric Crane No. DRT 81201 (previously numbered RDE1159/7) was based for several years at the small engineers yard just west of Carnforth station before being sold to the Ribble Steam Railway at Preston in 1997. It is pictured, paired with a former 13-ton Single Bolster wagon acting as a runner and an ex 22-ton plate wagon modified as a jib rest, at Preston in July 2018.

One of the last steam-powered cranes to remain in service was No. ADS 1826, TOPS coded ZZR, which had been built for the Southern Railway in 1943. With a lift capability of 10 tons it was eventually allocated to the M&EE's Power Supply Section at Horsham where it was used to lift electrical sub-stations and the like on and off the small fleet of Special wagons assigned to the Power Supply Section. Recorded at Horsham in July 1979, in company with its jib runner Flat ET No. ADB 907231, No. ADS 1826 would finally be withdrawn in 1986.

Both the Kershaw HOBC, and the later Plasser & Theurer MOBC and HOBC machines which would eventually replace it, operate with a rake of up to 18 bogie Single Line Spoil Handling wagons. These are each fitted with an onboard conveyor so that the spoil can be moved the full length of the formation filling up each wagon in turn, while the body of each wagon can be slewed to the side so that if required excess spoil can be transferred to a line of open wagons drawn up alongside. The HOBCs can cover around a mile-and-a-quarter of track during a single 10-hour possession, and once cleaned approximately 60% of the original ballast might be suitable for reuse. Some 45 Plasser & Theurer SLSH wagons were built between 1995 and 1999 including No. DR92260 pictured at Crewe Gresty Lane in June 2000.

In 1977 there were still more than 40 steam-powered cranes being operated by the Civil Engineers Department on tasks such as the replacement of track panels, switches and crossings, and for general yard duties. Included among them was No. DB 967330, a Taylor & Hubbard 15-ton Heavy Duty Steam Crane built in 1955. Allocated to Low Fell Engineers Depot it is pictured on track relaying work at Heaton South Junction in March 1977. Although some high visibility attire is evident among the track gang, hard hats are still few and far between. This crane would eventually be scrapped at Low Fell in September 1985.

Changes within the departmental fleet were not just confined to its wagons but also encompassed other on-track plant and equipment as more efficient methods of infrastructure maintenance and renewal were developed. Ballast cleaning, which involved removing all the ballast to at least nine inches below the base of the sleepers, then sorting it so that the good stone within size specification could be returned to the foundation and the rest discarded, had for many years been undertaken by BRs fleet of Plasser & Theurer RM62 and RM74 machines, but by the turn of the century many had either been withdrawn or mothballed with such work increasingly undertaken by new medium and high output ballast cleaning machines. P&T RM74 ballast cleaner No. DR76303 is pictured at Guide Bridge in April 1994 while Network Rail's Kershaw High Output Ballast Cleaner, No. DR76101 undergoes repair at Crewe Gresty Lane in July 2000.

In 1975 the Civil Engineers Department issued a new specification for a 12-tonne telescopic-jib diesel hydraulic Heavy Duty General Purpose Crane, now required to replace both its remaining steam cranes and also some of its older diesel cranes. In all some 44 new 12-tonne cranes were purchased, 30 from Plasser Railway Machinery (GB) Ltd and 14 from Clarke Chapman Ltd (Cowans Sheldon) with delivery being completed between 1978 and 1981. Each manufacturer produced its own design to comply with the specification, although the bogies, brake gear, engines, safe load indicators and ropes were common to both suppliers. When not operational the crane jib stowed within its own length for in-train or self-propelled travel, the cranes being able to travel under their own power at up to 15mph unladen or 1.5mph when towing a trailing load of 140 tonnes, while in train formation they could be hauled at up to 65mph. The Plasser cranes were allocated to the Southern and Western regions, as well as to the southern half of the London Midland and Eastern, while the Cowans Sheldon cranes went to Scotland and northern areas of the London Midland and Eastern Regions. Plasser 12-tonne Heavy Duty General Purpose Crane No. DRP 81527 (also numbered DB 969024) is pictured on a track lifting job at Horbury, near Wakefield, in May 1991.

In BR days each of the regions had its own plant maintenance depot, that on the Southern being located near to Ashford Pre-Assembly Depot. Painted in departmental 'Dutch' livery, Class 73 No. 73108 heads a short 7R84 10.18 Ashford PAD to Tonbridge West Yard working, comprising a Plasser 12-tonne crane and a ZDA (ex-OAA) through Ashford station on June 7, 1992.

A Smith Rodley Twin-Jib Crane is seen at work on the recently electrified line through Coventry station sometime in 1967. Developed for lifting timber sleepered track these early machines could lift from six to 10 tons, but most were not self-propelled requiring a locomotive to move them along the track. (©Trevor Mann collection)

In the early 1970s 14 former Warwell wagons were fitted with pairs of British Hoist & Crane jibs with a combined lift capability of 10 tons. Once again they were not self-propelled and No. DRB 78113, previously numbered TRM14, is seen in the formation of a Wrexham to Crewe engineers train at Chester in July 1986.

The disadvantage of the Twin-Jib Track Relayers is that possession of two tracks is required, while they cannot be used on single lines. Nonetheless in 1975 a total of 28 new Self-Propelled Heavy Duty Twin-Jib Track Relayers were purchased by BR with the order, like that for the Heavy Duty General Purpose Cranes, again being split between Plasser and Cowans Sheldon. Overall lifting capacity was 12½ tonnes, although each individual lifting unit was rated at seven tonnes to cater for any unequal weight distribution within the track panels. When not in use the crane jibs stowed within the length of the carriage, as seen in this view of No. DRC 78234 recorded at Tyne Yard on May 5, 2002. This was one of the 14 Twin-Jib Track Relayers built by Cowans Sheldon and it had recently been repainted in the short-lived Jarvis livery.

Following the privatisation of infrastructure maintenance nearly all such work was thenceforth undertaken under contract, either by newly formed companies made up of existing railway civil engineering staff, or by well-established general civil engineering companies. Consequently there was a move to even greater mechanisation of equipment, while the adoption of 60kg/m rail section and pre-tensioned concrete bearers in place of long timbers in trackwork turnouts, meant that the existing fleet of permanent way cranes was found to be inadequate. Therefore, in 2001 Grant Rail and Balfour Beatty each took delivery of a new telescopic-jib crane from the German manufacturer Kirow, designed to be able to lift 100 tonnes, or 27 tonnes when 'free on rail', that is with the jib in the horizontal. This facility is essential for when working under the wires, enabling the crane to pick up a turnout from a delivery wagon and move it to its final position. Balfour Beatty's 100-tonne Type KRC810UK crane No. DRK 81602 is pictured with two track panels at Barry in January 2014. (©Hywel Thomas)

To replace the twin-jib track relayers a new general-purpose 25-tonne crane was also devised by Kirow specifically for the replacement of track and smaller switches and crossings. They work either singly or in pairs with seven being introduced between 2006 and 2017 and, like their larger brothers, when in train formation they run accompanied by a runner/support wagon at either end. These provide both for the transportation of lifting beams but also to spread the axle-load configuration of the formation to achieve RA8 route availability. Kirow Type KRC250S crane No. DRK 81626 (also numbered 99709319012-9), with former bogie container flat No. TIPH 93330 in use as its beam carrier, is seen in the formation of a Toton to Crewe Basford Hall working near Crewe on April 17, 2019.

CHAPTER 17

I'm Special

BR inherited a number of Lowmacs from each of the 'Big Four' rail companies, including 80 Lowmac EPs built by the London & North Eastern Railway to LNE diagram No. 173. Like the Lowmac MOs, which had been built for the LMS by the LNER, the Lowmac EPs were vacuum-braked measuring 30ft over headstocks with a 16ft well and a 22ft wheelbase. They could carry 25 tons and No. LDE278483 was one of two Lowmac EPs that were fitted with Westinghouse through air-pipes for use in train ferry service between Harwich and Zeebrugge. However, when photographed at Northampton ACE Sidings in April 1995 it had been transferred to the engineers, recoded ZYW, and lettered 'ELECTRIFICATION B.T. WAGON'.

To meet their obligations as common carriers the early railway companies had built a wide selection of 'Specially Constructed Wagons' which were designed to carry large, heavy and often cumbersome loads. In addition to inheriting many of these 'Specials' British Railways would also build a considerable number of such wagons themselves, these often being copies of earlier designs simply updated with contemporary running gear, buffers and axleboxes. However, as the country's road network improved the movement of such loads by rail declined and by the late 1970s, aside from those few still being used to serve customers such as British Steel, the CEGB, the Ministry of Defence and the UKAEA, most of the remaining 'Specials' had been transferred to the departmental fleet where they found further use either as cripple carriers or carrying engineers' plant and other infrastructure equipment.

Most numerous among the specials were the Low Machine Wagons, two-axle vehicles in which the floor dipped in the centre so as to accommodate tall loads that would otherwise have been out of gauge. Codenamed Lowmac they were designed so that wheeled vehicles could be driven on and off from an end-loading bank and during the 1970s some could still be found in revenue traffic carrying military vehicles around the country. XLV No. M700700, a Lowmac MO, is pictured at Warrington Arpley when loaded with a Saracen armoured personnel carrier in October 1979. (©Trevor Mann)

The 20 Flatrol EACs, built by BR in 1959 to diagram 2/530, were also intended for train ferry service, being fitted with roller bearings, continental pattern self-contained buffers and label holders, vacuum brakes and a Westinghouse through air pipe. At 33ft 9in over headstocks with an 18ft 4in well they could carry 21 tons. By the early 1980s they were no longer required in cross-Channel use with six then being reallocated to the Power Supply Section at Horsham. Now coded ZVW No. ADB900118 (previously numbered 21 70 9096 012-1) was loaded with an electrical sub-station assembly when recorded at Horsham in June 1992.

The 40-ton capacity Flatrol MHH was also an LMS design being 58ft over headstocks with a 35ft 6in well. BR would build some 15 to diagram 2/511 with LMS-style diamond-frame bogies between 1949 and 1954, while a further 11 would be built between 1953 and 1957 to diagram 2/524 with plateback bogies. Coded YVR No. ADB900407, one of the diagram 2/511 wagons now fitted with a through air pipe is pictured at Ellesmere Port East Sidings in October 1993. It is loaded with a crippled Shell Class A tank wagon which had been damaged during a shunting accident at Jarrow oil terminal. Lettering on the Flatrol read 'CM&EE EMERGENCY/VEHICLE RETURN/TO CREWE/ETE SIDINGS/MAX SPEED/45 MPH'. Until the mid-1990s a pool of bogie Flatrols and Weltrols was used to remove badly damaged wagons from the site of derailments but today's damaged vehicles are either recovered by road or, more often, simply cut up on site.

The transport of mechanical equipment to the site of engineering possessions was also a common duty for many of the surviving special wagons. Here a pair of Flatrols deliver two diggers to an engineering possession at Poynton station, on the Macclesfield to Stockport line, in the late 1980s. (©Dave Millward)

Only nine Flatrol EABs were built in four separate lots, all to diagram 2/516, between 1950 and 1956. They were shorter than the Flatrol EAC at only 28ft 6in over headstocks with an 18ft well and when built were unfitted. Six survived in departmental use into the 1990s by which date they had been equipped with through air and vacuum pipes as seen in this view of ZVR No. DB900101 at Guide Bridge in April 1994. Its pale green panels identify it as one of the wagons assigned to 'Operation Clean Sweep', a local initiative to remove discarded sleepers, rails and troughing from the railway's right of way.

The Special Wagons fleet also included a large number of bogie Flatrols and again several pre-nationalisation vehicles could still be seen in use well into the 1990s. The Flatrol MR, an LMS design built at Derby in 1941 to diagram 97A, was 53ft 8½in over headstocks with a 40ft well and could carry 20 tons, with YYP No. LDM700370 one of two Flatrol MR to be transferred to the departmental fleet. Fitted with a through vacuum pipe it had been modified to work as part of the CM&EE Electrification Unit train based at Doncaster Hexthorpe when recorded at Ashburys Yard, Manchester, in March 1993.

BELOW: British Rail followed the example of the GWR and LMS in building both four-wheel and six-wheel Girder wagons. Carrying capacities ranged from 40 to 100 tons when operating in pairs and all the survivors had been transferred to the departmental fleet by 1983 where they were used to carry bridge beams and other lengthy loads. Named 'Conger' and TOPS coded YVO, Nos. DB998072 and DB998073 are seen at Healey Mills yard in May 1989. Built at Ashford Works in 1970 these were the last unfitted wagons built new by British Rail.

LEFT: Class 45 No. 45149, unofficially named 'Phaeton', heads a special working comprising the four BR six-wheel Girder wagons and two Brake Vans off the Erewash Valley line at Clay Cross Junction in August 1987. The girder load had originated from the nearby Butterley Engineering Co. *(©Trevor Mann)collection)*

Since the early 1960s Special Wagons have been used to move irradiated nuclear fuel from atomic research establishments and nuclear power stations to the reprocessing facilities at Dounreay, in Caithness, and at Sellafield on the Cumbrian Coast. Among the first wagons modified for this traffic were a small number of BR Rectanks, built to diagram 2/440 between 1958 and 1960, which were later fitted with various types of cradle designed to support either rectangular or cylindrical fuel flasks. Rectank WC No. B909039, one of four to be modified at Barassie C&W in 1965, is pictured at BREL Shildon Works in 1973 when lettered 'To Work Between Leith Docks and Thurso'. It is loaded with a 'Unifetch' flask, a type used to carry irradiated HEU (Highly Enriched Uranium) fuel elements, which were shipped to Leith from material testing reactors in France, Denmark and Germany en route to the United Kingdom Atomic Energy Authority's site at Dounreay. *(©Trevor Mann collection)*

The use of Special Wagons to transport plant and other ancillary departmental equipment declined dramatically following rail privatisation as most engineering work was thenceforth undertaken by contractors who preferred to use road/rail vehicles for delivery and on-site work. Built by P&W MacLellan in 1952 dual-piped Flatrol EZ No. DB900501, a wagon that could trace its origin back to a Great Central Railway design from 1912, is pictured out of use at Crewe Gresty Lane Engineers Yard in October 1999. Of note are its GCR-style diamond-frame bogies and unusual 'butterfly-style' wheel handbrake.

The first purpose-built nuclear flask wagons were the batch of 24 vacuum-braked Flatrol MJs constructed to diagram 2/532 at Swindon in 1963. Numbered B900509-32 they initially ran on six-wheel plate bogies and were used to carry Magnox fuel flasks from CEGB and SSEB nuclear power stations in Britain to Sellafield, as well as handling the occasional movement from Barrow Docks to Sellafield of flasks shipped from the Magnox power station at Latina in Italy. Measuring 49ft over headstocks, and with a carrying capacity of 50 tons, No. B900528 was carrying a flask sun-shield but no flask when photographed at the Shildon Works Open Day in August 1973. *(©Trevor Mann collection)*

By the late 1970s the vacuum-braked Flatrol MJs were becoming inconvenient to operate, particularly as they were unable to carry the 55-tonne glw flasks that had been introduced to carry spent fuel from Britain's second generation of nuclear power stations, the Advanced Gas-Cooled Reactors. Consequently in 1980 they were refurbished with strengthened frames, air-brakes and new FBT6 four-wheel bogies, as pictured in this view of No. B900511 seen heading north at Warrington Bank Quay in August 1986.

RIGHT: Irradiated nuclear fuel traffic increased considerably during the 1970s and a new design of stainless steel-bodied, 56-tonne capacity, air-braked flask wagon was introduced. Running on Y25C four-wheel bogies, some 51 Flatrol MJJs were built between 1976 and 1988 and FNA No. 550053 is pictured at Sellafield in May 2005.

In 2014 the Nuclear Decommissioning Authority, successor to BNFL, introduced an initial batch of 10 'new generation' nuclear flask wagons built by WH Davis, with a further 19 being ordered by 2018. All are fitted with SCT Barber BER 22.5 'Easy Ride' bogies and white painted sliding flask cover, but they differ from earlier flask wagons in having visible bodyside framing and are finished in blue livery. FNA No. 11 70 9229 013-1 was recorded at Carnforth when en route from Sellafield to Heysham Power Station in May 2017.

CHAPTER 18

While main line steam working ceased in August 1968, a number of industrial steam locomotives remained in use until the 1980s. Unsurprisingly the majority were to be found working for the National Coal Board, but a handful of other companies also continued to operate steam for a few more years. These included the British Aluminium Company's works at Burntisland, where its trio of saddle tanks remained in operation until 1971 when they were replaced by two Fowler diesel mechanical 0-4-0s obtained second-hand from the United Fireclay Products Co. of Bathville, West Lothian. The British Aluminium works at Burntisland produced alumina, receiving fuel oil in tank wagons and coal and bauxite ore both in 16-tonne Minerals; the bauxite being railed to the works from Burntisland Harbour. BACo. No 1, a Peckett 0-4-0ST, works No. P1376 built 1915, was busy shunting the works sidings at Burntisland in September 1969. This locomotive is now preserved on the Caledonian Railway at Brechin. *(©Trevor Mann collection)*

The Industrial Locomotive Scene

In 1968 standard gauge industrial locomotives could still be found working at more than 1000 locations across Britain, from large steelworks, collieries and chemical plants to small scrapyards and wagon cleaning facilities; but over the next half century that number would fall to less than 100. This decline in the use of industrials was driven by several factors, in particular the transfer of much traffic to road during the 1970s which saw many firms dispense with their internal railway sidings, while takeovers and amalgamations resulted in others concentrating their remaining operations at fewer works.

At the same time the number of industrial locomotive builders also declined, with several well-known names, such as Hudswell Clarke and John Fowler, having ceased to trade by the end of the 1970s. Not only had the demand for new locomotives slowed, but British Rail's decision to dispose of a large number of its smaller diesel shunting locomotives had further depressed the market. While no longer required by BR, due to the closure of many local goods yards and the diminished need for local trip workings, these locomotives were often still in good condition and could be purchased at a considerably lower price than a new locomotive. The general economic downturn of the early 1980s resulted in further cutbacks in rail activity and the decade would see several other long-established industrial locomotive builders either disappear or amalgamate with one or more of their competitors.

Subsequently privatisation of the coal and electricity generating industries, traditionally both major employers of industrial locomotives, brought about further fleet reductions, while since the late 1990s an increasing number of ex-BR Class 08 diesel shunters have found their way into industrial use. In particular the Class 08s have been popular with some of the locomotive hire firms that have sprung up since the Millennium, with many manufacturing and quarrying companies now preferring to concentrate on their core business activity and contract out their railway shunting requirements to a specialist concern.

The Corn Products Co. whose works in Trafford Park, Manchester, produced starch, also continued to use a steam locomotive to shunt traffic in and out of its premises well into the 1970s. Built by Andrew Barclay in 1929, the CPC 0-4-0ST, works No. AB1964, is pictured shunting 21-tonne Hoppers just inside the factory gates at the end of Trafford Park Road in April 1974. Inbound coal from Yorkshire for the works boilers remained the main rail traffic handled at CPC until a new combined heating and power system was installed in the early 1980s. After its withdrawal the CPC locomotive was first preserved at the Manchester Museum of Science and Technology, but since 1984 it has been based at several heritage sites, including the Foxfield Light Railway, the Chasewater Light Railway and the Lincolnshire Wolds Railway.

At locations where the use of a steam locomotive would have posed a hazard, such as chemical plants and paper mills, it had been common to employ fireless locomotives for internal shunting. By the late 1960s most had been replaced by diesels, but a handful of fireless engines remained in service for a few more years; indeed the last fireless continued to work at the Glaxo pharmaceutical plant situated on the outskirts of Ulverston until 1993. Laporte Chemicals was another company to operate fireless locomotives, with four working at its plant in Luton until 1971. The youngest of the fleet, works No. AB2243, built 1948, is pictured in preservation at the Buckinghamshire Railway Centre, Quainton Road, in July 1998. When at Luton its main task had been to shunt inbound tank wagons loaded with hydrogen peroxide from the BR exchange sidings to the unloading point within the plant.

LEFT: Many small concerns either closed or dispensed with their rail operations during the 1990s, but one such company to survive until 2002 was Jake Rail Tank Cleaning Services at Ellesmere Port. As its name suggested, Jake's main activity was tank wagon cleaning, both internal and external, and it owned a small Ruston & Hornsby 4wDM chain-driven locomotive to move wagons around the cramped site. Class 88DS works No. RH466626, built 1962, is pictured at Ellesmere Port in January 1994.

Rea Bulk Handling's main work involved shunting wagons at the Bidston Dock Ore Terminal, from where up to 10 trains a day of imported iron ore would be handed over to BR for onward delivery to the John Summer's steelworks at Shotton. The final two locomotives to be purchased new by Rea's were a pair of 32-ton 0-4-0 diesel mechanicals, which were ordered from the Drewry Car Co. in 1963 and built under contract by E.E. Baguley Ltd. of Burton-on-Trent. Fitted with a 195 bhp six-cylinder Gardiner 6L3B engine, the first of the pair, works No. Bg/DC2724 named 'Kathleen Nicholls', is pictured at Bidston Dock in September 1979. Stable behind 'Kathleen Nicholls' are 'Wabana' and 'WM Salthouse', two of Rea's Robert Stephenson & Hawthorns-built 0-4-0DM locomotives. Unfortunately by the early 1980s Rea's business was on the wane and following the cessation of the ore traffic at Bidston Dock, in 1981 the company wound up its entire rail operation. In addition to the sale of its sole Yorkshire to CC Crump & Co. the second of Rea's 195 bhp Baguley/Drewry locomotives, 'Dorothy Lightfoot', went to AV Dawson to work at its rail-served distribution depot at Middlesbrough. However, the remainder of the fleet would linger for several years in store at Birkenhead before eventually being scrapped in 1990.

Not all industrial concerns limited their locomotives to one supplier and Rea Bulk Handling, which was responsible for shunting the lines serving the docks at Bidston and Birkenhead, purchased a more diverse fleet with its 11 diesels being sourced from four builders: E.E. Baguley, Robert Stephenson & Hawthorns, Vulcan Foundry and the Yorkshire Engine Co. Rea's sole Yorkshire, a 200 bhp 0-4-0DE works No. YE2732 purchased new in 1959 and named 'Labrador' after the part of Newfoundland where iron ore was extracted, is seen at Bidston Dock in May 1979 when stabled for the weekend in company with 'Kathleen Nicholls', one of two Baguley-built 195 bhp 0-4-0DMs which Rea had purchased new in 1963. Also present were 'Theseus', a 150 bhp 0-4-0DM built at the Vulcan Foundry in 1951, and 'Pepel', a 204 bhp 0-6-0DM built for Rea by Robert Stephenson & Hawthorns in 1955.

Several companies have entered the locomotive hire business including Cotswold Rail, the Hunslet Engine Co., and RT Rail. Like most of them RT Rail specialised in hiring Class 08s and No. 08588, painted in RT Rail's rather plain black livery, was spotted shunting bogie hoppers at Dove Holes Quarry, Peak Forest, in July 2006. In 2007 EWS would later take over responsibility for shunting the quarry sidings and No. 08588 was transferred to the Bombardier works at Ilford, while in 2008 RT Rail was sold to British American Railway Services.

The North British Locomotive Company of Glasgow was one builder to close its doors during the 1960s, although this was rather down to its struggle to successfully manage the transition to diesel and electric locomotive production than prevailing market conditions. Among the last industrials built by the company were four 225 bhp 0-4-0DH locomotives supplied to the Cadbury chocolate factory at Bournville between 1959 and 1961. When rail traffic at Bournville ceased in 1976 all four were sold – works No. NB28038, built 1961, and the former Cadbury No. 15, being acquired by TW Ward Ltd of Briton Ferry. It is pictured at Briton Ferry's Norbrit Wharf in October 1994 where it was used to shunt steel coil traffic.

John Fowler of Leeds was another well-known builder with its range of small diesels proving very successful, but by the mid-1960s industrial customers were beginning to demand larger and more powerful locomotives and Fowler's ceased production in 1968. One of its biggest customers was the British Electricity Authority and its successor the Central Electricity Generating Board, and works No. JF4210001 was one of two Fowler Class 421 150 bhp 0-4-0 diesel mechanical locomotives built in 1949 for the BEA's Skelton Grange Power Station in Leeds. In subsequent years it was rebuilt with hydraulic transmission and transferred to the CEGB's Padiham Power Station, near Burnley, where it was photographed in August 1990.

Arguably the high point of industrial locomotive building in Britain was in the 1950s and early 1960s, when most manufacturers were working at peak capacity and among the most prolific of builders was Ruston & Hornsby whose Boultham Works in Lincoln turned out a range of four and six-wheeled diesel-mechanical and diesel-electric designs. One of Ruston's best customers was Colvilles Ltd., the Scottish steel producer, that purchased more than 40 0-4-0 diesel electric locomotives from the firm between 1956 and 1962 to shunt traffic at its steelworks at Clydebridge, Dalzell, Glengarnock, Ravenscraig and Tolcross. The Clyde Alloy Steel Co., a Colvilles subsidiary that produced hardened and high tensile steel at its Craigneuk and Hillside works near Motherwell, had already purchased four 0-4-0DE locomotives from Ruston & Hornsby and following the nationalisation of the steel industry in 1967 the former Clyde Alloy Steel No. 2, works No. RH323605, a 1954-built 165 bhp 0-4-0DE, was subsequently transferred to BSC's Hardendale Quarry at Shap where it is pictured, when stored out of use, in May 1992.

During the 1990s many companies chose to concentrate on their core business activities and began contracting out their rail operations to one of the locomotive hire firms that had been established. One of the earliest of these was Rail Management Services Locotec based in Dewsbury, that from 1992 offered not only traction for hire but also staff and track maintenance services to several concerns including Brunner Mond at Northwich and Mobil Oil at Coryton. In addition to the former Rea Bulk Handling 0-4-0DE Yorkshire the RMS Locotec fleet included a handful of former BR Class 08s, along with three 0-6-0DH Sentinel locomotives acquired from the closed British Steel Ravenscraig works. Refurbished and repainted in RMSL livery hire locomotive No. H012, previously British Steel No. 39, works No. RR10289 built 1970, shunts potash hoppers at Tees Dock in June 1996. RMS Locotec would later become a subsidiary of British American Railway Services based at Wolsingham on the Weardale Railway.

Diesel mechanical designs which were easy to maintain had dominated in the 1950s but by the mid-1960s technical improvements saw most industrial locomotive builders introduce diesel hydraulic models to their range. Hydraulic transmission provided a much smoother torque, particularly when shunting heavier trains, while other new design features that would become commonplace were dual-controls, to facilitate either side driving, and spacious cabs with large windows which afforded the driver with good all-round visibility. Wide steps at the front and rear of locomotives, on which the shunter could ride with safety, were also a feature of most designs by the early 1970s. In 1964 the Hunslet Engine Co. introduced a 0-6-0 diesel hydraulic powered by a Rolls Royce C6SFL 325 bhp engine which would become one of its most successful designs. The first of the type was works No. HE6294, which initially worked for the National Coal Board at Snibston and then Rawdon collieries in Leicestershire, before being sold to Goole Railfreight Ltd. Named 'Frederick J. Moate' it is pictured at Goole Docks in July 1992. Subsequently this locomotive saw service with the British Coal Opencast Executive at Coedbach and Cleveland Potash at Boulby.

Bigger wagons and heavier trains required larger and more powerful industrial locomotives to shunt them, but none came any larger than Foster Yeoman's No. 44, works No. 798033-1, a type SW1001 'switcher' built by General Motors at its La Grange works at Chicago, Illinois, in 1980. Named *'Western Yeoman II'* the 1000hp Bo-BoDE was some 44ft 8in in length with a height of 14ft 3in, a size that confined it to Merehead where it replaced a pair of second-hand 350 bhp Class 08s which, coupled cab to cab, had previously been used to shunt the quarry. *'Western Yeoman II'* towers over a rake of MBAs as it hauls them towards the loading sidings at Merehead on September 12, 2002.

Another quarry company to invest in a new powerful industrial was Tilling Construction, who in 1994 purchased a massive 150-tonne Co-Co diesel hydraulic from RFS Engineering at Doncaster. Based at Rylstone Quarry, north of Skipton, it was delivered in Tilcon's red livery but following the company's acquisition by Tarmac in 2001 it would be repainted. Named *'Cracoe'*, after the nearby village, works No. 067/C4498GA/57000/001 was the final locomotive to be built at Doncaster Works, just as RFS went into receivership, and is pictured when stabled between duties at Rylstone in June 2018.

In recent years the building of new industrials has slowed to a trickle but companies such as HNRC (Harry Needle Railroad Co.), Hunslet Barclay and the LH Group have remained busy rebuilding and refurbishing existing units, including a number of previously stored or preserved locomotives that have been returned to traffic after being fitted with new engines and electrical wiring. Works No. AB613 was one of four 0-6-0 diesel-hydraulics built in 1977 for the National Coal Board's North East Area, it later being based on the Bowes Railway at Gateshead. Subsequently rebuilt by HNRC at Barrow Hill in 2008 it was then leased to La Farge Cement and is pictured shunting PCAs at Hope Cement Works on June 1, 2019. By now ownership of the works at Hope had been transferred to Hope Construction Materials, as reflected by the small sticker on the side of No. 5's bonnet, although the locomotive retains the green and grey colours of La Farge.

CHAPTER 19

BR Brake Vans

In November 1983 Class 31 No. 31159 heads the daily Newton Abbot to Exeter Riverside yard trip freight near Starcross. The train consists of two Procor two-axle air-braked sheeted PGA hopper wagons, both carrying ball clay from the Watts Blake & Bearne siding at Newton Abbot and destined for PD Stirling at Mossend, and a 12-ton Vanfit which was in departmental traffic from Newton Abbot TMD. As the train was partially fitted, with the continuous brake in operation only on the PGAs, a Brake Van was required at the rear of the train.

Even when a train was fully fitted, if any of its wagons were loaded with certain dangerous goods, such as toxic gases or nuclear fuel rods, then a Brake Van was still required at the rear. This was so that, in the event of an accident, the guard would be in a position to go back along the line to carry out train protection without having to walk past the dangerous load. Class 25 No. 25257 slips behind the platform at Sandbach with 6T51, the 14.35 Speedlink trip from BP Chemicals' Elworth Works, Sandbach, to Crewe Basford Hall yard on April 16, 1985. The train comprises a single loaded liquid chlorine tank which was destined for Esso's Fawley refinery, while a BDA, an OBA and an OCA act as barrier wagons providing the requisite separation distance between the tank wagon and both the locomotive and the Brake Van.

Most ubiquitous of all freight rolling stock was the Brake Van and until 1969 they could be found bringing up the rear of almost every freight working. However, that year an agreement was reached between BR and the unions that a Brake Van was no longer required on most fully-fitted trains and thereafter their numbers steadily declined.

In 1974 there were still some 4400 Standard 20-ton BR Brake Vans registered on TOPS but by 1992 that number had fallen to just over 300. Furthermore, of those the majority had been transferred to the engineers' fleet with only 125 allocated to revenue service, mainly being available to accompany trains loaded with nuclear flasks or certain other dangerous goods. The final demise of toxic gas traffic in 1994, followed by the decision to dispense with Brake Vans on nuclear workings in 1997, reduced the number of Brake Vans in the revenue fleet still further and by 2004 no more than half a dozen were still in regular use as propelling vehicles. At the same time the entire departmental wagon fleet had finally become air-braked and by 2008 the need for Brake Vans had disappeared.

Although their use in revenue traffic declined rapidly from the mid-1980s, many Brake Vans could still be found in the departmental fleet. Repainted in engineers olive green livery, ZTO No. DB 953695 is pictured at St Helen's Shaw Street in April 1984.

A small number of Brake Vans ended their days as Staff Vans with some receiving quite distinctive liveries. ZPR No. KDB 950718 had been assigned to the BR Telecommunications department when recorded at Warrington Arpley in May 1992.

One of the last BR Brake Vans still in use was ZTR No. B955172 which had been repanelled and converted into a propelling van with the addition of warning horns and adjustable visors. It is pictured at Tees Yard on November 23, 2002.